WHEN DEAD KINGS SPEAK

Psychic stories featuring Royalty, Popes, politicians and statesmen . . . dead and alive!

GW00711492

TONY ORTZEN comes from a family of journalists. His grandfather, Robert Elder, worked for many years in Fleet Street while both his parents were at one time reporters on weekly papers. Tony followed suit and was indentured for three years on the award-winning *Bucks Examiner,* based in Chesham. He entered full-time journalism after studying history, sociology and economics at a College of Further Education.

Though seriously intending to enter social work, he became a journalist and in 1972 joined the London-based weekly *Psychic News,* which circulates in over 70 countries. He became editor in 1981, shelving plans to emigrate permanently to Australia to do so.

Tony had already a keen interest in psychic matters and the paranormal for many years. Since joining *Psychic News* he has appeared on BBC TV, BBC local radio stations, the World Service and commercial stations, and written for other publications, including *The Times* and *The Stage.* He has started research on another book, also with a psychic theme.

Apart from writing, travel is another of Tony's interests. In fact, he was one of the first Britons to visit the tiny Baltic state of Albania—then run along Chinese Communist lines—since the Second World War. Another of his interests is alternative medicine, particularly homoeopathy, which is based on the basis of like curing like. This method of complementary treatment is patronised by some members of the Royal Family, notably the Queen.

WHEN DEAD KINGS SPEAK

*Psychic stories featuring Royalty, Popes
and statesmen . . . dead and alive!*

by

Tony Ortzen

Regency Press (London & New York) Ltd.
125 High Holborn, London WC1V 6QA

ISBN 0 7212 0785 5

Printed and bound in Great Britain by
Buckland Press Ltd., Dover, Kent.

Acknowledgements

First, I would like to thank the Rev. Allan Barham for permitting me to quote from an interview with Eva Lees, the daughter of R. J. Lees, a medium consulted by Queen Victoria. I would also like to thank Jean Watson, who typed the final manuscript and made sense of various amendments and alterations to the original script. The material in this book has been drawn from many sources. I have, if necessary, tried to contact those whose findings I have consulted and sometimes quoted. Unfortunately, I was not able to locate all those individuals since their words were in various cases written decades ago. To all of them I owe a debt for making this book possible. Lastly, I would like to place on record my appreciation to Karl Duncan for his help and suggestions.

Front cover photograph. This appears by kind permission of Peter Moore, of the Imperial Collection. The crown is taken from the 180 piece collection of the Royal and the Imperial Crown Jewels of the World in replica. These are on permanent display at the Imperial Collection Exhibition, Central Hall, Westminster, London SW1.

Contents

List of Illustrations

Plates 6, 7, 9 and 10 are reproduced by kind permission of BBC Hulton Picture Library.

Foreword by Doris Stokes

I FIRST MET Tony Ortzen about ten years ago when he came to interview me for *Psychic News*. He seemed very young to me then and a bit shy, but full of enthusiasm. If I remember rightly I did a sitting for him and was able to tell him amongst other things that he was a twin. He was a bit taken aback as people often are when they first get proof that the loved ones they have lost aren't "dead" but living on on the Other Side and still taking an active interest in the family they've left behind. Tony went away, gave me a good write-up and we've been friends ever since.

These days Tony is the editor of *Psychic News* and takes psychic matters in his stride, but there are still a lot of people who don't understand what a medium does. Some expect me to tell fortunes: I don't. Others expect to find a weird lady in a caftan and hooped earrings sitting in a darkened room over a smoking candle. I think they must be quite disappointed when all they end up with is plain old Doris in her carpet slippers drinking a cup of tea!

Most of all though, even if they don't admit it, people think mediums are a bit strange. It's an attitude I'm quite used to. As girl in Grantham I was always getting a belt from my mother for telling lies when I came out with things I couldn't possibly have known in any ordinary way. My father, who was a Romany gipsy, was more prepared to take me seriously, but mum used to scold him for it. "Don't encourage her, Sam," she'd say. "She'll end up in a mental home."

At the time I used to try to suppress my psychic powers. Now, of course, I realise that it's all as natural as breathing. Everyone is born with psychic powers, although some are more gifted than others, but the more you use your psychic ability the more it develops.

I am clairaudient, a fancy name for being able to hear spirit voices. Some mediums are clairvoyant, which means they see spirit people.

Occasionally I can do both. When I was younger I would often see spirit people, but now I tend to see only spirit children. It must be old age creeping on!

But being able to talk to spirit people does not mean I can chat to anyone I choose. People are always asking me to have a word with Elvis Presley or President Kennedy, and I have to explain it doesn't work like that. Once, when I was being interviewed in Australia, a reporter asked, "What does it feel like to raise the dead?" "Raise the dead?" I replied. "I couldn't even raise the skin off a rice pudding!"

I cannot force spirit people to come and talk. They only come if they want to come; what brings them is the love they feel for the sitter. It is no good a sitter saying she wants to talk to John Lennon. If John Lennon has never met her on earth, why should he want to come back and talk from the Other Side? On the other hand, her old grandma who has watched over her since she was a baby is probably dying to come through for a chat.

The nicest thing about my job is that I get to meet so many lovely people. I think I've had sitters from practically every country in the world, from every walk of life from bricklayers to generals, from cleaners to film stars. I've met lots of famous people. Some, like Diana Dors and her husband Alan Lake, are sadly no longer with us on this plane; others, like Freddie Starr and Pat Phoenix, are still going strong, thank goodness.

However, one thing I cannot claim is to have given a sitting to any members of the Royal Family, even though I'm told quite a few know a lot about it. I agree with Tony when he says they too know what grief, tragedy and tears are all about. Grief is the price we have to pay for loving someone when they pass on . . . and that applies to everybody. Naturally I was glad to read about the Queen Mother sitting with medium Lilian Bailey, and that Prince Charles has a keen interest in many forms of what some call alternative medicine.

I've got a lot to thank doctors for, though, having suffered cancer more than once and undergone several operations. In fact, one of my friends joked that the spirit world was taking me over piece by piece.

It was also good to see my old friend Harry Edwards, the healer, mentioned. I'll never forget the day John, my husband, and I spent at his sanctuary, Burrows Lea, near Dorking, Surrey. I wasn't too sure what to call this world famous healer, so asked him. "Call me Henry, Doris," he said. "All my friends do." It's a moment I'll never forget.

I found it fascinating reading how he had given spirit healing to members of our Royal Family. It also caught my interest seeing Margaret Thatcher mentioned since we are both from Grantham in Lincolnshire. Whenever he chairs my London meetings Tony always says: "Grantham has produced two very famous people. One's called Maggie and lives in No. 10. The other's called Doris and lives in South London." Mind you, there's sometimes a boo now and again when Maggie's mentioned!

Writing of Prince Charles, I should also say I'm pleased he's so open-minded about spiritual matters not only because he's to be our next king, but because he's young.

At my meetings I get all sorts: mums, dads, grannies, grandpas, everybody, and a lot of young people. I'll always remember coming out of one stage door . . . and finding some punks waiting to see me. Then down at Brighton some lads had waited for hours and hours in the cold.

As you'll read, Queen Victoria too knew a good deal about Spiritualism, and even had her own medium. It's such a pity, though, that most of the records of their sittings were destroyed because the knowledge that life after death is a fact can help so many people.

You know, every week I receive thousands of letters. They come by the sackful. In fact, the postlady sometimes pushes them along in a pram there's so many! You see, we're all going to die. It's a bit like going to Australia. If you were going to emigrate there, you'd find out all you could about what to expect. Well, it's the same with the spirit world. As we're all going to be there one day, why not find out something about it?

Many is the time I've read letters from people who have read my books and I've cried, they're so sad. Death causes people so much needless unhappiness. My privilege is to be able to show people that their dear ones are still around them and do still care and can come back to prove it.

I think our Royal Family do a marvellous job and am happy that now more people will know about their psychic stories. Mind you, I wouldn't want their positions for all the tea in China!

Introduction

FOR YEARS OUR Royal Family have been kept in protective wraps. Picture, if you can, the austere-looking Queen Mary or the rigid, black-dressed Victoria, both of whom looked as though smiles never crossed their lips. Compare that sombre, stiff, overformal scene with today's relaxed shots of Princess Diana or Prince Charles romping on the lawn showing off their first-born to the world like any other blissfully happy and supremely proud young couple.

I believe this stark difference in attitude and protocol is a two-way traffic. Like statesmen throughout the world, Royals have come to realise that no longer can they live totally shielded lives, protected and cosseted from the outside world and to some extent divorced from reality and the average citizen. The public almost feels it has a right to know details that only twenty or thirty years ago would have been denied to them. Now despite his somewhat conservative, traditional background Prince Charles can champion alternative medicine and even strike at the very heart of orthodox treatment by mentioning his conviction in a message, as retiring President, to the British Medical Association. What leaders, either elected or hereditary, might once have said in private and over brandies to a close knit circle of trusted confidants can now be stated in public. No longer can fringe medicine be labelled the interest only of cranks for as you will read it intrigues and has the whole-hearted support of a future king.

In their official roles, Royals and world figures may seem public paragons of confidence and strength, but stating the obvious they, too, are human and have their weaknesses and worries about life . . . and death.

Today more than ever before the media have gained access to our premiers, princes and so on. Through radio, television and the press many aspects of their personalities and innermost beliefs which were once shrouded in mystique have opened up.

Not that many years ago Buckingham Palace went into a flurry of frenzied activity merely because one national Sunday newspaper stated in print that the Queen Mother had consulted a well-known society seer. One can only imagine the scenes both within Buckingham Palace and the harassed editor's office when the story broke . . . and was speedily denied. Bear in mind that a few years earlier a Dutch Queen almost lost her throne, it is said, and caused a constitutional crisis, simply because of her close friendship with a faith healer. Yet the monarch's intent was simple, honest and sincere, to try and correct an eye fault affecting one of her daughters.

So it is that never before have the lives—and loves—of Royalty and statesmen been the subject of so much scrutiny not only by experts and analysts, but also by ordinary folk. Powerful people induce powerful emotions within their subjects.

But despite the new-found access to the world's rulers it is sometimes difficult to obtain cast-iron details surrounding a public figure and his or her psychic story. That monarchs have consulted mediums can never be denied. A medium might well undertake not to divulge the contents of a sitting, but that a seance took place will almost certainly become public knowledge. Everyone, be it commoner or king, loves to listen to gossip, intrigues and such-like. So though all documentary details of Queen Victoria's sittings with a servant have long since vanished we know this is a fact . . . because a king admitted this was so. Not some tittle-tattling domestic, but a monarch.

In life only one thing is certain . . . all must die. This natural law applies to all, rich and poor, atheist and devout believer. None can cheat or prevent the law. Some may delay it by various means, by so-called youth rejuvenating diets and lifestyles, but that death will come cannot be avoided. Many, and this surely includes those highest in the land, have deep-seated fears about what, if anything, lies beyond the grave.

I believe life after death is a fact. Some will disagree, but probably even more will concur. Opinion polls throughout the world show that millions upon millions accept without a shadow of intellectual, philosophical or spiritual doubt that life is eternal, that it does not cease with physical death. Countless individuals have consulted mediums, clairvoyants and healers. The facts now show that among them one can include those of blue blood, and political figures whose names are known to all.

Naturally, even in these enlightened days it is not possible to interview a Royal Family member and say: "I hear you have consulted a medium. Is that really so?" Such an idea, appealing though it is, is a foolish and fanciful notion. But today details do leak out. By piecing together these fragments in a jig-saw-like fashion, by tracking down witnesses, reading other accounts, and generally adopting a sleuth-type approach it is possible that a picture slowly emerges to verify such a claim.

Happily some mediums left copious notes of their sittings with the famed. Nettie Maynard, an American medium, gave countless sittings to President Lincoln within the White House. Fortunately, Miss Maynard left a rich source of material concerning these seances. Moreover, some witnesses signed affidavits to that effect. Likewise, today's technology and the sheer effect of news boomeranging from nation to nation ensures that, for example, predictions concerning President Kennedy's tragic assassination were not only known in America but in other countries.

Some maintain that interest in psychics and the like is the province of gullible old ladies, sitting in the dark, anxious and literally praying for Other World communciation no matter how banal and pathetic. Now there exists documentary proof that both Russia and America spend millions of pounds annually on psychic research. Science has invaded the seance room to try and cull its secrets, and, it must be said, mainly for military and espionage purposes. Psychic research is not only respectable but respected.

Over the years some statesmen have kept detailed records of their supernormal experiences. One name springs immediately to mind, Mackenzie King, still one of Canada's most respected Premiers. King in his private diaries made no secret of his afterlife acceptance. Even today many Canadians will not know that during the dark, depressing, downtrodden days of the Second World War King consulted British mediums. Churchill knew. Indeed, he told one clairvoyant that she had better take care or she would be carted off to the Tower!

In a sense I have written this book for over a decade in that I have been collecting and collating material, at least on a mental level. As editor of a weekly paper devoted to Spiritualism and the supernormal I have immediate access to hundreds of thousands of cuttings. Within a few minutes I can discover what a leading figure said about a particular aspect of the paranormal. Because of my job I am privileged to have access to a rich source of seance and other material. Naturally, I also know some of the world's best mediums. Often I am told stories strictly off the record. I never break my word. If a story is not to be reported I never even write the words down. So, I must admit, there are some accounts concerning Royalty I have not included simply because it would involve breaking a given confidence.

What even I found surprising during the research and writing of this book is the fact that so many statesmen and Royals throughout the world have delved into the paranormal in some shape or fashion. Russia may be fiercely atheist, but the fact that one of its recent presidents consulted a psychic healer cannot be denied. The story went round the world. The healer in question became a celebrity within Russia and enjoyed luxuries denied to the ordinary Soviet citizen. And though the Roman Catholic Church still officially frowns on mediums and spirit world contact there is evidence aplenty that more than one Pope knew a great deal about the subject.

It is also worth pointing out that interest in psychic matters knows no cultural or geographical boundaries. Within this book are accounts concerning countries as far apart politically and culturally as Britain, America, Russia, Canada, Nepal, France, Greece, Holland, Belgium, Poland and Persia. One common link emerges: their leaders have at one time or another consulted psychics or had their own supernormal experiences. Gifts of the spirit and paranormal incidents know no nationality bars. They are innate faculties given to mankind irrespective of race, religion and, it must be said, an individual's morals, character or intent. Perhaps that is why psychic phenomena often appear to be frustratingly elusive: accepting that there is a higher power he—or it— must surely realise there are those who would seek to abuse and prostitue these time-attested gifts to the detriment of all humankind.

Perhaps this also explains why psychic phenomena are so elusive within a laboratory or scientific surrounding. They cannot be summoned up or demonstrated to order. Neither can anyone raise the so-called dead. They return in the seance room because of vital links of love and friendship, ties which nothing, not even death, can sever. Moreover, bear in mind that psychic phenomena are repeatable in the sense that they have been witnessed in all centuries and all cultures.

I feel it is only fair to reiterate my belief in an afterlife. That does not mean I have lost a critical faculty and am all-believing. Indeed, probably the reverse is true. Because of my experience in the psychic realm I possibly tend to be over-cynical. Having seen some of the best seance room happenings available I can now judge the worst, the suspect, the possibly bogus. Thankfully, the number of charlatans operating is minimal.

One problem I did encounter was that some of the mediums mentioned in this book have long since died and passed to the world they did so much to champion for decades. As earlier explained, some left public record of their dealings with Royalty and statesmen. Others did not, but their stories and claims often live on in the shape of trusted relatives and friends who were able to supply details of meetings with world rulers. I have no reason to doubt their authenticity. Many of their accounts have an unquestionable ring of truth about them. Unscientific as it may sound, one soon develops a gut instinct, a sort of sixth sense, about whether to believe a story or not.

I will also admit that some of the accounts within this book may appear slightly sketchy and brief. Some might have been tempted to pad out such incidents in the hope that colourful language and length would somehow add to their authenticity. However, this I refuse to do. I do not like high-on-drama, low-on-fact tales. Stories, no matter how short, must stand on their merit and the facts available, no matter how few.

Recent years have seen a sexual revolution which would have horrified our Victorian ancestors. But we, too, have our taboo subjects, one of which is death. It is interesting that the last decade or so has seen an explosion of psychic matters. Indeed, writer Arthur Koestler left his not inconsiderable fortune to found and fund a Chair in Parapsychology—a fancy name for psychic research—at a British university. His bequest, incidentally, was eventually awarded to Edinburgh University.

Now read why I believe that the famed have consulted their dead loved ones, that they, too, have breached the gulf of so-called death. I maintain that kings, and others, can speak . . . whether dead or alive.

I hope having read this book you will, too.

Tony Ortzen

A Right Royal Rumpus

AT FIRST GLANCE Queen Victoria and the Queen Mother would seem to have extremely little in common. Victoria, a somewhat dumpy and often grumpy looking figure dressed in black, looked solemn, stern and unapproachable. The Queen Mother, on the other hand, with her pale blue eyes, pastel-coloured dresses and winning smile exudes a warm, reassuring aura of kindliness, comfort and genuine interest in all she meets.

Yet the pair share a central link: both were—or have been—widows for many long and possibly lonely years. Moreover, both were devastated when their beloved partners died. Victoria plunged into grief and hid from public view. The Queen Mother, her sorrow undoubtedly none the less, adjusted at least on the surface and eventually renewed her public life with increased vigour, determination and strength. Today she still reigns supreme in the hearts not only of Britons, but millions throughout the world. Her character and qualities appeal to those of all ages and beliefs. Even self-confessed anti-monarchists find their feelings wither and waiver in matters concerning the Queen Mother.

Yet Victoria and the Queen Mother share another less well-known and publicised link. Both have consulted mediums, those vital links between this world and the next. Furthermore, the Queen Mother was once at the heart of a Right Royal Rumpus which even today remains a mystery and will probably never be answered. The puzzle is this: did she or did she not seek guidance from a leading society seer? At all events it caused a flurry of excitement—and subsequent denials—which reverberated throughout Britain.

The seer in question is still practising. Today Tom Corbett continues to see the famed, fated and feted at his Chelsea, SW London, home. At the time of the Queen Mother's claimed sitting he was offered 'fabulous sums' to tell his story. He did not and still will not. 'I denied it then,' Tom told me, 'and I'll deny it now.'

The Royal row began after the old *Sunday Pictorial* in proverbial publish and be damned mood printed a story that Tom had been called to Clarence House to give the Queen Mother sittings. Within a few days the paper was forced to deny the story.

Much-read journalist Hannen Swaffer claimed in his eagerly read *World's Press News* column that the *Pictorial's* editor, Colin Valdar, 'insists' the account 'is true.' What's more, the paper stated that Corbett as well as visiting the Queen Mother was a well-known visitor to Princess Margaret.

When Corbett arrived by taxi, said the *Pictorial,* he was taken to the Queen Mother and read his crystal ball for her. 'Why does the Queen Mother consult him?' it asked. 'The marriage problems and prospects of Princess Margaret are a natural field for this crystal gazer.'

Corbett told the newspaper, 'I have always been more or less right about the Princess.' Then he added: 'I am afraid I cannot—indeed I must not—discuss any of my clients. Crystal gazers, like doctors, have a code of ethics.'

The newspaper said that 'Corbett was first taken to the Queen Mother by a lady-in-waiting. Since then he has been summoned to Clarence House about a dozen times. Royal patronage prompts his interest in the current problem of the Duchess of Kent. Is Princess Alexandra old enough to marry now—or should she be asked to wait a year? Is it true that he has an even more important client?'

Corbett would not be drawn further. 'Please don't ask me to discuss the matter,' he asked. The seer regarded it as a great honour to the whole profession to be called to Clarence House. Tom, who was then 41, had recently set up as a professional clairvoyant in Westminster. He had also given psychic readings in a night club as a cabaret attraction. Soon he was to face a denial of the story from Buckingham Palace. A spokesman said of the *Pictorial's* account: 'The whole report is untrue and fictitious. The denial applies to all members of the Royal Family.'

The paper stood by its published account, saying it had been checked and double-checked. Nonetheless, it subsequently devoted a whole front page to the 'Royal denial' which was illustrated with a photograph of Corbett arriving by car at Buckingham Palace the previous Wednesday.

The newspaper began by saying that its front-page story on the previous Sunday had prompted a denial from Buckingham Palace, which the *Pictorial* deeply regretted, and a subsequent denial from Corbett.

'As these challenge the accuracy and integrity of this newspaper,' it said, 'the attention of readers is invited to the Palace statement and to the following sequence of events.'

Its report was printed after three separate interviews with Corbett in the week before publication. At these interviews, experienced journalists examined and cross-examined Corbett on statements and admissions made by him.

The printed report was read over to Corbett on the Saturday evening. He made only one amendment, the withdrawal of a reference to the Duchess of Kent, which therefore appeared only in the very early editions.

Then followed the Palace denial: It read, 'The Press secretary to the Queen wishes to inform editors that the story concerning the crystal gazer visiting Queen Elizabeth the Queen Mother at Clarence House is untrue.' Immediately this was received, said the *Pictorial,* it re-examined Corbett on the telephone. He confirmed once again that the story he had seen printed in one of the final editions was entirely true.

On the Monday, Corbett was seen again by assistant editor, Rex North, who wrote the original story, and another journalist. Corbett offered to produce the evidence of date and times to substantiate what had been printed. He repeatedly confirmed the accuracy of the story.

On Tuesday, Corbett agreed to take all confirmatory evidence to the *Pictorial* office at 6.00 p.m. the following day. On the Wednesday morning, the *Pictorial* received a letter from the Queen's press secretary stating:

'(a) that Queen Elizabeth the Queen Mother does not know Mr Tom Corbett and, to the best of her belief, has never met him and, until your article appeared, had never heard of anybody of that name.

'(b) Mr Tom Corbett has never been summoned to Clarence House by Queen Elizabeth the Queen Mother, or by any person acting on Her Majesty's instructions.

'(c) It is untrue that Queen Elizabeth the Queen Mother has ever consulted Mr Tom Corbett.'

At 1.30 p.m. the editor and assistant editor, Rex North visited Corbett at his home. Again repeatedly he confirmed the accuracy of their printed story. But he added. 'In view of advice I have been given I feel I must not now give the confirmatory evidence to you. I will readily give it to Commander Colville (the Court Press secretary) at the Palace.'

In Corbett's presence the editor immediately telephoned Commander Colville, who agreed to see Corbett at 6.00 p.m. Just before 6.00 p.m. Corbett was photographed entering the Palace. He kept the appointment and saw Commander Colville, who had legal representatives with him.

After the visit Corbett told a journalist his version of what had happened and agreed that this should be reported to the editor.

Briefly, Corbett said that he had satisfied the Palace on all points. Commander Colville, stated the *Pictorial,* entirely repudiated this. The newspaper added that Corbett also indicated that 'he would now have to appear as a liar rather than cause further trouble to Palace circles.' He was going to consult a solicitor.

On Thursday at 6.00 p.m. Commander Colville told the *Pictorial* editor that the Queen's solicitor had advised him that a letter was on the way from Corbett's solicitor to the *Pictorial.* The letter to the editor arrived by hand at the newspaper office. It contained a categorical denial of the article on Corbett's behalf.

Corbett's solicitors issued a statement to the Press which said they had been instructed by him to state that the reports contained in the *Sunday Pictorial* that he had been consulted by the Queen Mother and the Duchess of Kent were untrue.

The *Pictorial* account ended: 'This newspaper, in accepting the Palace denial and as evidence of good faith to our readers, has felt it necessary to give publicity to the above.' In a panel was printed: 'The *Pictorial* would never knowingly publish any inaccuracy. Above all, an inaccuracy which could cause distress or embarrassment to Queen Elizabeth the Queen Mother. It greatly regrets the sequel to this recent publication.'

What cannot be denied is that the whole, strange, story hit a raw nerve at Buckingham Palace. For it issued its first swift denial at 1.15 p.m. on the day the scoop story appeared. As for Tom Corbett, so worried was he, the seer did not sleep for forty-eight hours.

Why was the story denied? The reason for it, according to the old *Daily Herald,* was: 'As Head of the Church of England, the Queen must take seriously a suggestion involving the Royal Family with a man claiming to have occult powers. The Palace remembers the constitutional crisis in Holland two years ago over Queen Juliana's use of faith-healer Greet Hofmans.'

Today Tom Corbett's lips remain sealed, but not those of company secretary Gordon Adams, the former son-in-law of Lilian Bailey with whom, he and others assert, the Queen Mother attempted, and successfully, to contact her dead husband.

The sittings, Gordon told me, occurred with Mrs Bailey, OBE, in secret. Monarch and medium were introduced through Lionel Logue, the Australian speech therapist.

Gordon continued: 'Mrs Logue, who had recently passed, gave remarkable evidence to her husband who must have mentioned this to King George VI at one of their periodical therapy sessions.

'The King once remarked, "My family is no stranger to Spiritualism," and told Logue of Queen Victoria's diaries relating to her sittings with John Brown, all of which were destroyed except one, by the Dean of Windsor, Dr Randall Davidson, and which had been found in the archives at Windsor.

'Later, Mrs Bailey was asked to accompany a lady to give a sitting to a group of VIPs. Mrs Bailey at first declined saying she did not give sittings to groups of people. Later she was persuaded and was accompanied by a mysterious lady who asked if Mrs Bailey would mind being blindfolded. She agreed and was taken to an unknown address and blindfolded.

'She heard a rustle of skirts as the sitters took their places and then went into trance. After the sitting was over, the blindfold was removed —and Mrs Bailey found herself facing the Queen Mother and other members of the Royal Family. These sittings were repeated a number of times, but no blindfold was used.

'All requests were conducted through a lady-in-waiting, although on one occasion a phone call was received by Mrs Bailey at her home in Wembley, Middlesex, from the Queen Mother speaking from the Castle Mey, her home in Scotland. At this time the Dutch press were up in arms over the matter of Queen Juliana consulting faith healer Greet Hofmans.

'At the last sitting Mrs Bailey gave to the Queen Mother, the Queen Mother took off a gold brooch from her dress and gave it to Mrs Bailey. "It is of no real value," she said. "We own very little jewellery ourselves. It belongs to the nation, but I would like you to accept this."'

So what did her husband, George VI, know about seances? A lot, it would seem. Again the central figures are medium Lilian Bailey and speech therapist Lionel Logue.

The Australian, who died in 1953, made no secret of his Spiritualism. Indeed, he told the King about the remarkable evidence for survival after death he received through Lilian Bailey, the medium with whom he sat once every month for seven years.

Logue remained 'one of the King's closest friends,' said the *Daily Express* at the time, which added, 'The names of the two men are inseparable.'

Part of Logue's psychic story was revealed by Hannen Swaffer. It all began when he approached Swaffer after the passing of his beloved wife which caused such a gap that he even contemplated suicide.

His first seance was held in Swaffer's flat. Mrs Bailey could not have known Logue's identity because his portrait had not appeared in any newspapers. The journalist did not mention Logue's name to the medium.

Almost at the beginning she was embarrassed because she could see the spirit form of King George V. 'He asks me to thank you for what you did for his son,' said the medium. To her surprise Logue answered, 'I quite understand.'

At his second sitting with Lilian Bailey, Logue received evidence that completely convinced him. Her spirit guide, William Hedley Wootton, inquired, 'Is there any question you want to ask?' Logue answered, 'Does my wife want to say anything about the place where we first met?'

Wootton, when he answered, said with a puzzled expression: 'She is referring to a bird named Charlie. It is not a canary. It looks like a sparrow.'

This overwhelmed Logue. Charlie Sparrow was his best friend. It was at Charlie's 21st birthday party that he met the future Mrs Logue and fell in love with her.

Logue put another question. 'Does she remember the place?' The guide answered, 'It was Fre . . . Fremantle.' Charlie Sparrow's house was in Fremantle. This evidence so impressed Logue that time and again he mentioned it to Lilian Bailey.

Through this medium, his wife told him that he must not dream of taking his life because it would only divide them. At that time the medium did not know that the thought of suicide was in Logue's mind.

His wife continued, at successive seances, to show detailed interest in all that concerned her husband. When he moved from a large house to a flat, he asked one day if she could remember what had happened to the bed linen. Immediately came the answer that she wanted him to use the yellow sheets and pillow cases; she described the box where Logue later found them.

These monthly sittings were held either in Mrs Bailey's home or later, when he became ill, at Logue's flat in Knightsbridge. Lilian Bailey stated that of all the sitters she met she seldom knew of a husband and wife so devoted to one another.

It was Logue who told her that Spiritualism enabled him to understand his work of correcting speech defects which occupied the major part of his life. He realised that he had been guided to leave Australia, when there was no apparent reason, to seek a new career in this country.

Without knowing why at the time he had sold up his home. There were no seeming prospects in Britain and it appeared to be madness. Through his seances, he realised that he had come to London in order that he could cure the grave defect in the speech of the man destined to be King.

Lilian Bailey was convinced that Logue was a natural psychic. This was borne out by the fact that he instantly knew what was wrong with the patients who consulted him.

Having received his conviction of Survival, Logue's life was transformed. On many occasions he told King George VI about his seances and never, it was said, met with hostility.

After the King's passing Logue received several messages from him through Mrs Logue. He was asked to transmit one of these messages to Buckingham Palace. This Logue always hoped to be able to do when his health improved, but his long illness confined him to his home. In his last twelve months he underwent five operations.

Logue was so grateful to Lilian Bailey for the comfort and proof she had brought him that when one of her grandsons was to be named (Spiritualism's alternative to Christening) at the London Spiritual Mission, Pembridge Place, he acted as Godfather. And in his will he left Lilian, who was awarded her OBE for secretarial services during the First World War, a very special chair— the one used by George VI when he attended the speech therapy treatments.

Though it may never be clear whether the Queen Mother consulted society seer Tom Corbett or not, it was never denied that members of the Royal Family had consulted Nell St John Montague, who described herself as 'the well-known society clairvoyante.' When she was invited to the wedding of the Duke of Kent in 1934 her publicity agent broadcast details of the ensemble she would wear.

To return to earlier times, Britain and its empire was shattered in 1861 when Prince Albert died. Queen Victoria, mother of nine, a devoted wife and monarch, was grief-stricken. Yet within months the so-called dead Consort proved he was very much alive by speaking through a teenage boy, one who later became a famous journalist and part-time medium to the Queen.

'I will be good,' said the monarch on ascending to the throne. Indeed she was. Britain prospered. As the industrial revolution gathered speed, factory chimneys spouted through Britain, changing the face of town and country. There was prosperity for the few, but slums for many. Votes for all was a thing of the future and votes for women quite unthinkable.

Yet over all Britain and many parts of the world where the Union Jack proudly flew one woman ruled supreme. Victoria. Like Britain she was revered or feared. Britons truly never would be slaves; Britannia and her gunboats really ruled the waves.

When Victoria married Prince Albert of Saxe-Coburg in 1840 it was a blue blood love match. Her husband, stated the Queen, was 'perfection in every way, in beauty, in everything. Oh, how I adore and love him.' Sadly the two were only to know twenty-one years of married life . . . at least on this side of the veil. For in reality Queen Victoria, though nicknamed the Widow of Windsor, was as close to her husband in death as in life. Nothing, not even physical death, separated their lives. For years after her beloved Albert's death Victoria slept with his nightclothes in her arms. Some say that during four long decades of widowhood she never went to a theatre or concert, attended or gave a court ball.

Victoria ruled a staggering sixty-three years, seven months. Though today little remains in the way of documentary proof concerning Queen Victoria's psychic life, it is certain that soon after she became sovereign Victoria presented a gold watch to a medium. The engraved inscription read, 'Presented by her majesty to Miss Georgiana Eagle for her meritorious clairvoyance produced at Osborne House, Isle of Wight, July 15th, 1846.'

So did the Queen personally summon Miss Eagle to Osborne House?

With whom was contact made? How many other Royal personages were present at these psychic sittings? We do not know. What is fascinating is that Victoria was certainly interested in matters supernormal two years before the advent of modern Spiritualism in America in 1848. So proof exists that before table-turning and spirit world contact became a fashionable Victorian vogue, Victoria was at the heart of it. What sparked the monarch's interest in Spiritualism we do not know. Certainly it was not Albert's death. The date of her sittings with Miss Eagle prove once and for all that Victoria was investigating mediumship while Albert was most definitely in the flesh.

Today, however, mystery surrounds the watch or its exact whereabouts. The watch is believed to have been returned to the Queen on Miss Eagle's death, but no one truly knows. What can be ascertained is that it eventually came into the possession of W. T. Stead, a noted and campaigning journalist probably best known for his role in fighting child prostitution. Stead later presented the watch to an American medium, Etta Wreidt, in whose presence the dead actually spoke. In her turn Mrs Wreidt, when she reached the ripe old age of seventy-six, gave it to the former London Spiritualist Alliance. For many years it was displayed at the College of Psychic Science, now the College of Psychic Studies.

Without doubt thousands throughout the world saw the watch and wondered. It is interesting to note that Mrs Wreidt handed over the watch after sending it to the Duchess of Hamilton. It was she who suggested that the Alliance was a suitable home for the historic time piece. Sadly, the watch was stolen some years ago and has never been traced.

But how many other seances did the Queen arrange on the Isle of Wight? No one knows the answer. It was definitely more than one. Sittings were undoubtedly held at the cottage of Mrs Cust, a famous medium of the day. It seems that at one session the young Prince Imperial Louis Napoleon literally acted the ghost . . . and one can assume the Queen was not amused!

Sitters, including the Prince and Princess of Wales, saw furniture dance and heard objects thrown about when lights were dimmed. When they were raised, however, the incorrigible young Prince Imperial was found to be responsible for the phenomena.

Banished from the room the funster waited for the seance to resume then 'manifested' again with much rustlings, patterings and stroking of cheeks. Somebody struck a match. In its flickering, eerie, light the Prince Imperial was seen in his stockinged feet, carrying a large bag of flour! On yet another occasion the Prince of Wales decided to lend a hand at one of Mrs Cust's seances by 'materialising' a live donkey through the windows of a guest room and putting the animal to bed.

Amusing as these incidents may seem, Victoria was undoubtedly serious in her psychic interests, and even more so after her devoted Albert passed on. That in turn led to an even greater mystery which even today still causes fierce controversy: was John Brown, her faithful, brusque, whisky-drinking servant her medium?

Brown, whom Victoria called 'God's own gift,' certainly had an astonishing hold over the Queen. After his death Victoria wrote *A Biography of John Brown* which she circulated privately. Friends persuaded her not to publish it. Moreover, the Queen personally designed a John Brown Memorial Brooch which boasted the servant's head on one side and the Royal monogram on the other. It was made in gold.

Not surprisingly the unlikely rapport which developed between a rude servant and a monarch who ruled all she surveyed and more could not be kept entirely quiet. Indeed, the radical press went as far as to call Victoria—and quite openly—Mrs Brown.

After her husband's death, a clergyman suggested to the all-powerful widow that she should consider herself married to Christ. 'That,' replied the Queen in forthright manner, 'is what I call twaddle.' Victoria knew otherwise. She believed her husband, though physically dead, was in reality still alive, that he was merely one rung of the ladder ahead, in the spirit realms.

Sadly the one person who could offer oral evidence to support this claim has died. But before her death the woman in question, Eva Lees, was questioned by a vicar, the Rev Allan Barham. He tape-recorded an interview with Miss Lees, then aged over eighty, a few years before she died.

Miss Lees explained quietly and faithfully how her father, Robert James Lees, became Queen Victoria's first medium and how John Brown became his successor. 'My father,' she stated, 'was born a psychic. He could remember that when he was two-and-a-half after they had put him to bed they could not leave him in the room without a candle alight until he saw a Scotsman beside him. Now, he came from a Scottish family well back and a Scotsman used to come and sit beside his bed and he'd say, "You can take the candle and leave me alone." They didn't know why, exactly, because they thought it was a childish fancy.'

When young Robert reached the age of seven, his father had a growing family of several children. Robert was number three.

'My grandfather,' Miss Lees explained, 'wanted a cheap house and he got one at the bottom of the lane, but they told him it was haunted. So he said, "Haunted or not, if any of the devils come near me, I'll soon get rid of them."

'Well, they got settled in. There was a great deal of trouble and noise on the staircase, disturbances they didn't like. My father had an elder brother, William, and his father said, "William, will you sit up with me and we'll watch the staircase tonight?" William said, "Yes, Father." They got no results at all, although they sat well on into the morning.

'The next night grandfather said he'd sit again so my father said: "Can I sit? I didn't like being alone in my bedroom last night. I didn't sleep." His father said, "Yes, if you won't be frightened." Well, he sat in front of the door which was wide open and watched the top stairs.

'About one o'clock, all of a sudden he went deathly white and fell unconscious on the floor. They put him on the bed. He didn't come round until four o'clock. Then they said, "What was the matter, Jimmy?" He said: "I saw a little boy, about as big as me, coming down the top stairs in a white nightgown. When he got four stairs from the bottom he lifted his head and blood came right the way down over his nightgown." That gave him the shock which made him unconscious.'

Young Jimmy's father asked him if he would sit again. The next night the same apparition was seen. It went down the stairs, around the kitchen and behind the door leading to the cellar. Father and son followed the ghost. The pair made their way to the top end of the cellar which went under the roadway. Then the spirit form disappeared.

Next day they dug up the floor. Found was a skeleton of a little boy aged about eight. Police checked their records and discovered that a man and woman had lived at the house . . . with a young boy. The couple claimed he went missing. So heartbroken were they the parents went to America. 'But,' said Miss Lees, 'they had murdered the boy and buried him. That was my father's first experience. And it was a horrible one.'

Within a few years Spiritualism came to Britain. The Lees family, in common with many others, started to experiment with table-turning.

Using this somewhat cumbersome and slow method, communication can be established with the dead.

Soon after the Prince Consort died, the Lees were holding one of their regular table sessions. Young Robert—known as Jimmy to the family—asked if he could join in. Permission was given.

Miss Lees filled in some more details. 'My grandfather,' she added, 'was a terribly violent tempered man. They sat at the table. All of a sudden my father went sleepy. He kept shaking himself to keep awake because he was afraid his father would be violent. At all event he dropped right off. Well, he found out afterwards it was two hours later when he woke up. His mother was crying.'

The boy medium asked what was wrong. 'I could not help it,' he assured his father. 'I could not keep awake.' Doubtless fearing a quick clout across the ear, Jimmy was reassured when his father replied: 'Never mind, boy. Don't you know what you've been saying?'

'No, father,' said the child. 'I went to sleep.'

'Well,' his father replied, 'what you told us we never told you children, that our first baby was a boy that died twelve hours old, when we lived in Nuneaton. You have been talking to us and told us you were that baby of ours.'

The family knew little of Spiritualism. Jimmy's elder brother, William, went off and told his Bible Class leader, Aaron Franklin, about the seance. Mr Franklin attended one of the next seances. Again Jimmy was entranced by a spirit being.

Franklin was so impressed he contacted the editor of *The Spiritualist*, the first Spiritualist newspaper, edited by a man named Burns. And when he attended he, too, heard the dead Prince Consort speak.

One can only imagine the excitement Burns felt. Here was a story . . . and what a story. It is the kind of sensational scoop journalists long for and dream about, the return of a dead Royal Family member. Burns printed an account in *The Spiritualist*. Moreover, he sent a copy to Victoria.

A week later, said Miss Lees, Franklin turned up to another seance with two total strangers. Assured they were all right, the sitting began, and what a sitting it proved to be. Jimmy was again entranced by Albert. 'I am pleased to see you here, Lord so-and-so,' said the voice from the lad's lips. 'You are Lord so-and-so and your friend is the Earl of so-and-so. You have come from the lady respecting what was given last time.'

Eventually, the strangers admitted they had been sent on a Royal errand, to see if it really was the Prince Consort communicating from beyond the grave. Would he, through the medium, write a message—they did not mention the Queen's name—and sign it with his own private signature used between the two of them?

'And he did,' said Miss Lees. 'The Prince Consort came through. He got up—my father was only fourteen—and went and shook hands with the highest Masonic sign in England to prove to these two gentlemen—they both belonged to the same Lodge—who he was. They took the message. They then came back and said she, the Queen, wished to see him. Would the boy go back with him? Well, my grandfather was agreeable, but it was not for my grandfather, nor was it for my father. It was the messenger from the Other Side who was using him.'

Jimmy's spirit guide, a sort of guardian angel appointed to all on this earth, sent a message stating: 'We cannot let this boy come. He has work to do in this life that no other soul can do. But if she will send to Balmoral a youth named John Brown, who used to be on the golf course with the gentleman in question, he can communicate to her through John Brown. We will help that. But only under exceptional circumstances when the necessity arises and the Prince Consort cannot get through, can she send for him.' This of course, referred to Jimmy.

'Whenever we saw the carriage and pair and two gentlemen arrive,' said Miss Lees, 'we knew where he was going and what he was going for. Nothing was ever said in our family at all about it.'

Victoria, Miss Lees continued, sent for her father shortly before she died. The ageing sovereign asked: 'What can I do for you? You never let me do anything for you.' Lees, who never took a penny from the Queen, explained he was working for God and that He would look after him.

'Well,' the Queen replied, 'I am going to the Isle of Wight and I shall never come back. I hope God will reward you.' Lees told the monarch, 'If I have done for my Queen what my God wished me to there's nothing more to be said.'

Later in life Lees became a journalist and author of some note on psychic matters. Married in 1871 he joined the *Manchester Guardian* two years later and helped to launch *Tit Bits*. Friendly with two other powerful figures, Gladstone and Disraeli, it is claimed that Victoria once ordered six specially bound copies of one of Lees' psychic books. These she presented to members of the Royal family.

So what of John Brown, the surly servant? Had her seance records remained intact, they would have provided incontrovertible proof in her own handwriting that the Queen definitely did establish Other World contact with her dead husband.

Sadly, so little remains to verify the part John Brown played in Queen Victoria's psychic life. That she gave him medals cannot be disputed. In 1965 three of these were sold at Sotheby's for £550. Neither can it be disputed that Victoria had a firm belief in contact with the spirit world. Indeed, in 1901, the year of her death, the *Leeds Daily News* reported that the Queen was 'a devout believer in spirit communion and derived the greatest comfort throughout her widowhood from it. She was conscious of the supporting presence of her beloved husband in many critical periods of her life.'

A few years earlier the *London Daily News* printed a letter from the monarch in acknowledgement of the gift of a Bible from 'many widows.' She replied: 'Pray express to all these kind sister-widows the deep and heartfelt gratitude of their widowed Queen . . . To her the only consolation she experiences is in the constant sense of his (her husband's) unseen presence and the pleased thought of the eternal union hereafter, which will make the bitter anguish of the present appear as naught.'

What is certain is that when Brown died suddenly in 1883, the Queen's grief was as great as it had been when her devoted husband died. Interestingly, when the Queen died, King Edward VII smashed a number of memorial statuettes of Brown with his own hands.

On the amusing side, however, when Disraeli lay dying—and he it was who winkled Victoria out of mourning—the Queen sent him flowers and messages daily. Towards the end she asked if she might come and see him. It is said that the weak, tired face turned and Disraeli said: 'No, it is better not. She will only want me to take a message to Albert.' But that, as we have already seen, was hardly necessary. From the evidence available it seems that Queen Victoria already had a direct link to the Other Side . . . and to her husband. But has Victoria returned since her passing? Here are the facts.

Her daughter, Princess Louise, was convinced by many communications received through London medium Leslie Flint, who has now retired.

One sitter at a seance held by Leslie, retained his anonymity—until his identity was disclosed by a spirit communicator. Announcing herself as Lady Camperdown, she addressed the recipient as James.

The man revealed he was John James who, in his youth, was footman to Lady Camperdown. His next post was as house steward to Princess Louise at Kensington Palace.

James became one of Leslie Flint's regular sitters. Victoria once thanked him for giving healing to her daughter. A natural healer, he many times relieved Princess Louise's arthritic pain.

The Princess asked for a meeting to be arranged with Leslie. For more than an hour they chatted about his work and the evidential messages the Princess received from her husband and her royal mother.

Another of Leslie Flint's communicators was John Brown. A tape was made of the gillie's broad Scots accent as he said: 'When I had associations with this cult I can say I never broke my trust. Lots of people disliked me intensely. Some thought I took great liberties and wrote things trying to give false impressions.

'Her Majesty was always kind and good and had great respect for me. People in high places tried to suppress things . . . but it's not for me to talk about that now.' He added: 'We were very close in this work. She had to keep it dark.'

Neither is Queen Victoria the only monarch to make a well-attested spirit return.

Her eldest son, Britain's King Edward VII, communicated to Lady Warwick, always in German.

She told *Psychic News'* former editor, Maurice Barbanell, that once, at Warwick Castle, she noticed a seance trumpet standing on the floor. A megaphone-like device, these are used to amplify spirit voices.

'I picked it up and immediately I heard the voice of my old friend, King Edward, talking in German,' she testified.

At that time American medium Etta Wreidt, was visiting the castle.

'Whenever I sat with Mrs Wreidt,' added Lady Warwick, 'I always heard King Edward's voice, always speaking in German. He was so persistent that I got no other results, so I left off sitting.'

It is also worth recording that King Edward received warning of his impending passing eighteen weeks before it occurred. One night at dinner he turned to his neighbour, the Countess of Fingall, and told her he wanted a private word later. After the meal, he led her to a quiet corner of the drawing room. With deep solemnity he said, 'Lady Fingall, your friend Mrs Jameson has hurt me very badly.'

Mrs Jameson, a sister of Earl Haig, often received messages from her 'dead' brother, George, via automatic writing.

The King told Lady Fingall: 'She knows how much I loved my sister. She has written to me giving a message, which she says is from Alice.'

The King repeated the communication: 'The time is short. You must prepare.'

The startled Lady Fingall, realising the message's meaning, asked if there was any proof that it came from Princess Alice.

'Yes,' replied King Edward. 'She said I was to remember a day when we were on Ben Nevis together, found white heather and divided it.' He could see no way in which Mrs Jameson might have learned of this incident.

Later it emerged that not long before Edward's passing in 1910, his wife, Alexandra, invited a London medium to Windsor. Unknown to the King, a seance was held in one of the castle ante-rooms. A dozen sitters heard remarkable messages. One foretold the early death of the King in the house of his birth, and the outbreak in a few years of a great war.

When the Queen was holidaying in Corfu the following year, she was told Edward was not feeling well. Despite being reassured his condition was not in the least serious, she immediately left for home.

Alexandra arrived at Buckingham Palace—the King's birthplace—in time to see her husband breath his last. And she lived to see the First World War. She passed in 1925.

Queen Alexandra, it seems, was also psychic to a degree. Once she saw in her dressing room at Windsor Castle 'a tall woman in a black and white dress' standing at the doorway. The Queen also told a close friend she often heard supernormal music and singing during the night.

It is also said Queen Alexandra attended a voice seance with John C. Sloan, a Glasgow medium. The Controller of her Household had received at a Sloan seance some remarkable evidence from King Edward VII which he passed on to the Queen. This led the Queen to attend a Sloan voice seance.

'Yes, I remember the sitting she had with me,' said Sloan, when he was asked. 'She was so bonny and looked so young. You would have taken her for a young woman in her 30s!' Sir William Barrett, the famous scientist, who was present, told Sloan that she was over 70 at the time.

Further details were given by leading Spiritualist Arthur Findlay in his long out of print autobiography, *Looking Back*. Findlay was approached by the Hon Everard Fielding, an active member of the Society for Psychical Research, who said that a friend of his was coming to Glasgow. Could a seance be arranged for him with Sloan? Findlay said he would arrange it.

The man, a complete stranger, duly arrived. He dined with Findlay before the seance, giving no hint of his occupation. Findlay deliberately asked for no details. Thus no one at the seance knew anything about him.

The visitor was addressed correctly by a spirit voice, speaking clearly and distinctly. When he asked who was communicating, the voice replied, 'When on earth I was known as King Edward VII.' A personal conversation followed, the spirit voice naming people whom the recipient knew.

After some conversation between them, the voice said: 'I must thank you for all your kindness to my wife, Queen Alexandra. I do not know how she could have got on without you, and you have relieved her of much worry and care.'

When the seance was over, Findlay asked the newcomer if he was satisfied with his experience. He replied, 'Most certainly.'

Findlay's next question was, 'Will you tell me what your position is toward Queen Alexandra?' He answered, 'I am the Controller of her Household.'

When Queen Alexandra heard about the seance, she wanted to sit with Sloan. This was arranged in London. Findlay did not say what spirit messages the Queen received but the sitting, he said, 'gave her great satisfaction.'

Charles Speaks Out

MOST HUMAN BEINGS have a certain measure of free will. Taking background, personality, intelligence and natural talents into account, many can shape their lives, set goals, achieve them, and enjoy a lifestyle of one's choice. This does not apply to all. Some individuals are born into a role or have a destiny to fulfil which denies them complete freedom. Their futures lie in their family's past. Little can be done to alter events. Even wealth, no matter how great, can do nothing to buy their freedom.

Prince Charles is such an individual. From the moment he was born he has been groomed to be King. Every aspect of his life comes under scrutiny. Traditionally, and probably frustratingly, the Royal Family does not comment openly on politics and such matters. By and large Royals steer well clear of controversial subjects. Robbed of the power past monarchs wielded, their role in modern life is to act as figureheads, to bind the nation together and appear as focal figureheads who, unlike politicians, are not subject to electoral whims.

Despite his conservative background, however, Prince Charles has in a sense breached the book of protocol by speaking out and openly supporting alternative medicine which even today some doctors regard as hocus-pocus, the very domain of the weak, foolish and gullible. Nonetheless, it is widely believed that the British Medical Association's investigation into complementary medicine is in no small measure due to the Prince's passionate interest in unorthodox treatment.

The Prince, who it is rumoured is no stranger to a partially vegetarian way of life, made his views more than clear when he retired as the British Medical Association's president. Because of an engagement 'on the other side of the Atlantic' he was unable to be present at its annual general meeting which met in Dundee. Instead he sent an address. Part of it read: 'Don't overestimate the "sophisticated" approach to medicine. Please don't underestimate the importance of an awareness of what lies beneath the surface of the visible world and of those ancient, unconscious forces which still help to shape the psychological attitudes of modern man.

'Sophistication is only skin deep and when it comes to healing people it seems to me that account has to be taken of those sometimes long-neglected complementary methods of medicine which, in the right hands, can bring considerable relief, if not hope, to an increasing number of people. I hope that, while maintaining and improving the standards with which the Association is so rightly concerned, the medical profession will at the same time keep a corner of its mind open enough to admit those shafts of light which can preserve that sense of paradox, so vital to our sense of unity with nature.'

Later the Prince fired another broadside at orthodox medicine when he opened a Bristol Cancer Help Centre which offers so-called alternative treatments. Charles told those present he had 'looked forward very much' to visiting the centre. Having done so he was 'greatly impressed.' This was a result of 'meeting several of the patients and those who do the counselling and the treatment generally.'

The Prince admitted that for the first time in his life he had been wired to a bio-feedback machine 'which, much to my relief, reveals that my stress level was not as high as I thought it might have been.' The invitation to Bristol, he explained, came as a result of his British Medical Association address. Prince Charles continued: 'As a result of that speech, in which I urged the medical profession to look again with open minds at some of the principles that motivated Paracelsus and to treat the patient as a whole rather than purely mechanistically, I received an enormous number of letters, the vast majority of them expressing support for what I had been saying. Amongst the letters was one from the Bristol Cancer Help Centre which emphasised that the centre was involved in putting into practice the principles I had mentioned. I had no hesitation whatsoever in accepting the invitation because I wanted to find out for myself about the methods that are used in this centre. I must admit, before I go any further, that I am psychologically predisposed towards an acceptance of the very real possibilities of the value of such treatment as is offered here.

'I say this because I know that there are many others whose psychological make-up does not allow them to accept that such treatment, which cannot necessarily be proved in the objective scientific manner, has any value at all. But simply because a programme of therapy on three levels, physical, emotional and spiritual, such as is practised here, cannot be proved in a clinical laboratory to have any value to a patient, who anyway is far more than just a clinical specimen himself, does not mean that it is completely worthless or, for that matter, harmful.

'The great value, it seems to me, of the type of treatment provided here is not that extravagant claims are made on its behalf, but that it does no positive harm to the patient; far from it, for so much depends on marshalling the psychological and spiritual forces of the patient to tackle the appalling afflictions which have arisen. But marshalling these resources together with those remarkable ones belonging to Mother Nature are not carried out in direct competition with what could be termed as the orthodox approach to treating the patient but in a complementary sense.

'From my own personal point of view, I think it is only right that a patient should be free to try a different form of treatment if he or she feels that little progress is being made in, for instance, what may be referred to as a drug-based form of treatment. This alternative may involve a completely different form of diet, coupled with a better appreciation of the role that vitamins play in keeping our systems working properly. There are many people who have benefited from such an alternative approach to the treatment of their illness and I dare say, most of us here today have personal knowledge of friends or relations who have experienced such an alternative approach.'

Prince Charles added that apart from changes in diet and vitamin intake, there was one fundamental factor which seemed to be of 'crucial importance. That is that there are some wonderful, naturally gifted people about, several of whom work here I know, who can help those of us who find ourselves suffering from the terrible diseases that exist, in this case cancer, by altering our entire approach to life and, indeed, to death.

'Through their inspiration and through their love it is possible, I think, to achieve new attitudes, fresh hope, sometimes renewed determination to fight the disease every inch of the way, because no one can say with certainty that a cancer is fatal.

'Such an approach may be given any number of descriptions; it may be described as psychotherapy, or religion, or the power of prayer, or whatever, but it represents that invisible aspect of this universe, which although unprovable in terms of orthodox science, as man has devised it, nevertheless cries out for us to keep our minds as open as possible and not to dismiss it as mere hocus-pocus, for it can mean so much to those whose inner lives may be transformed through contact with these extraordinarily gifted people who we find here.'

Prince Charles added he could not speak from personal experience, 'but from what little intuitive sense I have.' In declaring the centre open, he hoped he 'could in some small way encourage doctors and healers to work together towards their mutual goal of healing the sick.' Not surprisingly complementary healers were jubilant. It seemed to them—and others—that alternative therapies had at last received a Royal seal of approval.

Others maintain that Prince Charles has delved further into the world of the paranormal and tried to contact Lord Louis Mountbatten, his much-loved Uncle Dickie, who was murdered by political terrorists. As far as I am aware, Buckingham Palace has never officially denied the story.

The first claim that Charles and Prince Philip had used a ouija board was made in the London-based *Spiritualist Gazette*, which is edited by a friend of mine, Tom Johanson. After the front-page story also appeared in *Psychic News* several national papers featured the account. Again, Buckingham Palace did not deny the charge. Indeed, when Pam Riva, assistant editor of *Psychic News*, contacted the Palace press office she was merely told by a spokeswoman she 'had no details' of the alleged ouija seance.

The *Gazette* headlined its story, 'Prince Charles' in the occult frightens Diana.' When this was read to the press officer, she commented 'I don't think there is any question of her being upset.'

In his account Tom Johanson said that Prince Charles' interest in spiritual healing 'has spread to psychic phenomena in general, including the ouija board.' Not only was this interest 'outraging' certain Church officials and many Church followers but 'terrifying' Princess Diana. Tom added that reliable Palace sources revealed the Queen was not amused 'because Prince Charles is over-stepping the traditional rule that the Royal Family should remain neutral concerning all controversial subjects.' It was reported Prince Charles had confided to a friend he wanted to hold a seance to contact Lord Mountbatten.

Tom continued: 'He has often stated to the Princess he strongly senses the presence of his uncle who he is convinced is anxious to communicate. Despite Diana's protests and great fears, he is determined to go ahead. Already both he and Prince Philip have made several experiments with the ouija board. Apparently, Charles' interest in what he calls "the spiritual dimension" was sparked off with the murder of Lord Mountbatten.'

A story from inside the Palace claimed that the future monarch would spend considerably more time experimenting with the spiritual world 'if it wasn't for his other commitments.' Furthermore an unknown confidante of Prince Charles said that when he and his wife visited Lord Mountbatten's home for a charity ball, Prince Charles is alleged to have said, 'When I dance with Diana it was as though Uncle Dickie was guiding me around the dance floor.'

In his account, Tom said that for Princess Diana the thought of Prince Charles 'being constantly followed around their home by the ghost of Uncle Dickie is too frightening to think about.' Nonetheless, Charles was eagerly collecting books on paranormal subjects and is determined to convince Diana.

Tom's story stated that in a letter to the Principal of the University of Wales, Prince Charles urged it to contend for author Arthur Koestler's massive bequest towards establishing Britain's first Chair in Parapsychology.

Prince Charles wrote this letter soon after details of the bequest were announced. He asked the college to apply for the cash. The idea was given full approval by the college senate.

Writing in her regular column for a national Sunday newspaper, Lady Olga Maitland had already reported that the Prince became 'deeply interested' in spiritual healing several years earlier. His mentor, with whom he held lengthy discussions, was Dr Mervyn Stockwood, the former Bishop of Southwark. Dr Stockwood has sat with mediums and praised survival evidence.

Lady Maitland said the Prince became friendly with the Bishop through Princess Margaret and Princess Alexandra, both of whom know Dr Stockwood well. Princess Alexandra's husband, Angus Ogilvy, has suffered for years from a painful back condition. He has consulted various spiritual healers.

An anonymous friend close to Prince Charles commented to Lady Maitland about Prince Charles' healing interest. 'It is a world which he has gone into in some depth,' said the acquaintance. The Prince was 'very aware that conventional medicine is often deeply suspicious of healing. But Prince Charles is also aware it would be stupid to ignore it.' At that time, a Buckingham Palace spokesman said it never commented on speeches made by Royal Family members. 'All I can say,' he explained, 'is that Prince Charles writes his own speeches.'

A few weeks later Tom Johanson returned to the same theme. The *Spiritualist Gazette* reported Earl Blancarthet as saying, 'Charles is very definitely creating a problem in the family by insisting on the infallibility of working things out by psychic methods.'

Tom added: 'Whilst a worried Princess Diana wisely accepts occult matters might influence certain important situations in life she is not so enthusiastic as her husband over the idea that it should play a big part in their lives. The fact is that Prince Charles is such an avid researcher in all aspects of the psychic field and is speaking so openly about it that many within his group of close friends refer to him as the "Prince of Psychics".' This 'jibe' followed disclosures that Prince Charles put pressure on the University of Wales to establish a Chair in Parapsychology.

The *Gazette* claimed that a number of meetings took place between Prince Charles and Dr Winifred Rushford, a leading expert in psychotherapy. Furthermore, it was stated that Dr Rushford's daughter, Dr Diana Bates, had 'several meetings with the Royal couple.' The meetings, it was said, were arranged by writer Sir Laurens van der Post.

Certainly two of Prince Charles' show-biz friends, Peter Sellers and Michael Bentine, have both sat with mediums and spoken more than once at Spiritualist gatherings. Michael Bentine represented Prince Charles at Sellers' memorial service. This was held at St Martin-in-the-Fields Church, London. Mr Bentine drove to the service direct from Buckingham Palace and sat alone on a front pew on behalf of the Prince.

The Prince, a great fan of the Goons radio programme, asked Bentine to be his personal representative. Another engagement prevented him from attending the service. After the service, Bentine, accompanied by well-known clairvoyant Doris Collins and her insurance broker husband Philip, drove to Buckingham Palace to report what had occurred to an equerry for the Prince's benefit.

But does Charles know that Broadlands, where he and the Princess of Wales stayed on the night of their marriage, was the scene of many a Victorian seance? This historic house, the home of Earl Mountbatten, was once owned by Lord and Lady Mount-Temple.

The full story of the sittings that were held there was unearthed by Professor Van Akin Burd and concerned John Ruskin, the artist, critic, man of letters, philosopher and social reformer. The professor, who has been involved with studies into Ruskin for over thirty years, presented the details when he delivered the Guild of St George Ruskin Lecture for 1982. It was given at London's Tallow Chandler's Hall.

Subsequently, the lecture was published as a booklet. In his acknowledgements, Professor Burd said that four years earlier Earl Mountbatten 'learning of my interest in Ruskin's relationship with the Mount-Temples, invited me to visit his home at Broadlands. Soon afterwards the trustees of the Broadlands archives gave me permission to study the Mount-Temple papers.' Lady Mount-Temple turned to Spiritualism, despite being taught the evangelical view of the Gospels, after her mother's death in May 1861.

Furthermore, though I cannot publicly reveal the name of the spirit healer concerned nor the very famous location, there is another psychic snippet concerning Uncle Dickie. A group of famous people spent an evening discussing the paranormal. The healer said Earl Mountbatten, a member of the Ghost Club, showed far more than a surface knowledge of psychic matters. He expressed his conviction of survival after death and added that his wife accepted reincarnation.

Charles, of course, would not be next in line for the throne had not The Abdication occurred. Though I have found no documentary proof to verify her assertions, British medium Bertha Harris maintained publicly—and more than once—to have told American divorcee Wallis Simpson she would never be Queen.

Over the years Mrs Harris made various statements concerning herself, Royalty and statesmen. Among these was Queen Mary, for whom she claimed to have transmitted spirit messages from her husband, George V. Other famous personages whose patronage she is said to have enjoyed were King George VI, Sir Winston Churchill, General de Gaulle and King Constantine and Queen Frederika of Greece.

According to Battling Bertha, she met King George VI many times. But never would she divulge what took place at these alleged sittings. 'That would be breaking faith,' she said. 'Secrets are safe with me. I can only tell you he came to me for advice about a lot of things.' However, Bertha stated she gave sittings to Mrs Simpson, later the Duchess of Windsor, one so near but so very far from Royalty.

Mrs Simpson 'never liked me after I told her she was in for a big shock the next day, something to do with embroidered underwear,' said the veteran medium in 1976. Bertha told Mrs Simpson that she had been to a famous store, ordered a wedding trousseau and given instructions to embroider the Royal cypher on everything. Seemingly unimpressed by her sitter, blunt Bertha—and she was certainly that—stated: 'They won't let you use the cypher. What's more, you will never be Queen of this country.' Later, the story goes, Mrs Simpson told the medium that the next day the store telephoned to say they could not carry out her orders.

According to psychic researcher and author Peter Underwood—he is president of the Ghost Club—many of her famous sitters, Bertha told him, 'were ashamed they consulted a clairvoyant and would park their big cars around the corner from her house and, collars turned up and hats pulled well down, would hurry to her house so they would not be recognised.'

De Gaulle, Bertha maintained, also sat with her. 'He had one great love for one person, his daughter, who had died of polio,' said the medium. 'I could make him happy by getting in touch with her.' Bertha, a minister of the Spiritualists' National Union, asserted she told de Gaulle during the war he would return to a Liberated France and become its leader. He would, however, give up his office, but then be asked back to make France strong again. His job would then be finished. Did this mean he would die? She told him it looked like that. His reply, Bertha explained, was, 'I will be ready as long as my country is free.'

What other details are available to support this sensational psychic story? Sadly, few. Bertha always stated she met the French leader at a country house party where among the other guests were Churchill and King George of Greece. De Gaulle was 'very diffident' when he called, with a French Embassy diplomat, for his first sitting. A devout Roman Catholic, he asked Bertha to keep quiet the fact he was attending seances. She kept the secret until the statesman died.

Mrs Harris always said that after her first sitting with de Gaulle, he said to her, 'I think I should send you some chocolates.' With rationing in force this could have been difficult, but the promised chocolates materialised without help from any spirit agency. De Gaulle obviously had more down-to-earth contacts as well.

The day following his death, the French President's biographer,

Pierre Galant, spoke on BBC Radio. 'Anne (his beloved daughter), was mongoloid', he explained, 'but he always used to speak with her and play with her, like the others.' When the child died, his wife Yvonne, cried bitterly. 'Why are you crying Yvonne?' the general asked. 'Don't you know that she is now like the other children?'

Hands That Heal

IN RECENT YEARS spiritual healing, which is basically simply the laying-on of hands or ministration through prayer, has achieved a status which even only a few years ago would have seemed totally impossible. Now spirit healers are allowed to treat patients in hospitals. Furthermore, doctors can recommend spiritual healing to their patients, provided they retain overall control. Until the last decade or so doctors ran the risk of being struck off the register if they took such a course of action.

It is only fair to state that doctors are still divided on the subject. Some believe spirit healing can play a vital role in the fight back to full health. Others dismiss it as being fraudulent or purely psychological in its benefit. However, what can be stated with utter certainty is that some Royal Family members have received spirit healing.

It was in 1956 that for the first time in British history court circles officially recognised a spirit healer. This was the world-renowned Harry Edwards, who during his long ministry received literally millions of letters from all corners of the globe. Today, his chosen successors Ray and Joan Branch continue the great man's work at his Burrows Lea, Shere, Surrey, sanctuary.

Edwards for six years secretly and successfully treated Princess Marie Louise, the oldest member of the Royal Family when she passed on at the age of eighty-four. A grand-daughter of Queen Victoria, she was great-aunt to the Queen. Subsequently, the healer was invited to attend her funeral service at St George's Chapel, Windsor Castle. The invitation, which specified that a seat had been reserved for him, was an indication that his services to the Princess had been recognised.

Edwards' healing commitments made it impossible for him to attend the funeral. He knew it would be the Princess' wish for him to devote his time to healing rather than attending the service. By arrangement with the Lord Chamberlain's office the healer's secretary represented him. Discreet about the role his healing hands played in connection with Royalty, Edwards seems not to have given full details till after the Princess' death.

Princess Marie Louise first consulted Edwards in 1950. She was suffering from arthritis of the right shoulder, elbows, hands and knees. The shoulder was most seriously affected, showing partial locking.

'At her first visit, the arthritis was taken away,' said Edwards. 'Her shoulder became free and she could move her knees without pain. It pleased her to demonstrate the healing to her personal friends by swinging her shoulders and moving her other joints. Apart from some inconvenience in her thumb joint, she never complained again about arthritis.'

The Princess always went to the sanctuary with her lady-in-waiting. She made a special appointment to go to Shere two days before the Coronation, to receive strength to help her through the long service and arduous Court functions.

'Similarly,' said Mr Edwards, 'she sought our help to enable her to carry out a tour of South Africa.' On her return she requested an appointment to express her thanks.

'The Princess would seek our help for all her friends who were sick, including names which I cannot disclose,' said Edwards. 'The first thing she would do on arriving here would be to relate the improvements which had taken place.

'I remember her concern for her relative the Queen of Spain, and her joy in telling me how the Queen had got so much better in the week following the commencement of spiritual healing for her.

'The Princess was the first member of the Royal Family to seek our help. Later came others associated with other families of reigning monarchs. Among them were two daughters of the King of Greece.

'There is little doubt that Princess Marie Louise discussed spiritual healing with many notable people. She sent me telegrams asking healing for sick friends, and through her ladies-in-waiting regular reports of her own progress and of any special needs she had.'

Princess Marie Louise visited Shere for the last time only a month before her death. 'It was obvious that her age was taking its toll,' said Edwards. 'She was so weak that she had to be assisted into the drawing room by her lady-in-waiting and her chauffeur. She was too weak to take the few further steps into the sanctuary itself.' At that time one of

Edwards' assistants was another noted healer, Olive Burton, who still practises healing in the locality.

Edwards continued: 'The Princess told us that all she wanted was strength to live a little while longer to see her autobiography published. After we had helped and given her strength, she was able to get out of the chair unassisted. She walked about the drawing room, and indeed, walked out to her car. She had her last wish. Not only did she live to see her book published, she was able to attend the literary lunch given in her honour.'

The next day when the Earl of Athlone, a great-uncle of the Queen died, Edwards revealed that three years earlier, at the request of members of his family, he had given him successful treatment after a severe nervous attack brought his condition so low that doctors gave up hope for his recovery. 'This restoration was freely credited to spiritual healing by Princess Marie Louise and other members of his family,' the healer stated. Later, Edwards claimed he was treating two other members of the Royal Family. When asked if any more were to receive his help, he replied: 'As a matter of fact there is one coming next week. Naturally, I cannot mention her name.'

What can now be mentioned is that Princess Marie Louise was also given spirit messages. The person responsible was Margaret Gordon Moore, a well known Spiritualist author. Her husband, a distinguished medical man, was Physician in Ordinary to Princess Beatrice, aunt to Princess Marie Louise. Though sceptical and critical by nature, Dr Moore was convinced through his wife's psychic powers.

She introduced him to well known medium, Estelle Roberts. Soon, her guide, Red Cloud, and he became firm friends. Once when a maid in the doctor's house was taken to hospital suffering agony from cancer, Dr Moore asked for the guide's help. Red Cloud said the servant unfortunately could not be cured, but he would stop all her pain, which Dr Moore thought was impossible without drugs. Nevertheless the maid had no pain for a fortnight, until she died peacefully.

The doctor made no secret of his seances to Princess Beatrice and to Princess Marie Louise, who frequently asked him to obtain from Red Cloud spirit messages from people she knew. This the doctor did and passed on the messages which, it is said, were always accepted.

Mrs Gordon Moore, a natural psychic from birth, recorded dramatic happenings through her mediumship in two books. Her mother appeared to her about twelve months before each of her children was born, giving the exact dates of their births. When her husband passed on she showed no trace of mourning, saying, 'I am quite ready to go.'

Intriguingly Mrs Gordon Moore once played a psychic cloak-and-dagger spirit-message role in another royal mystery. It concerned King George V. Few know that the King himself had first-hand experience of matters paranormal.

One spring morning in 1881, deckhands on HMS *Bacchante* were enjoying the calm seas. Suddenly, about 200 yards away, bathed in a red glow, they saw a phantom brig sailing towards them. The startled officer of the watch believed a collision was imminent. Yet, as he stared, the mysterious vessel vanished as suddenly as it had come.

The incident was recorded in the ship's log. Soon a knock was heard at the captain's door. A young cadet asked permission to copy the log entry into his diary. The cadet was the future King George V.

The monarch was no stranger to psychic happenings. When a *Psychic News* reader forwarded a spirit message from his mother, Queen Alexandra, he was surprised to receive a personally written letter of thanks signed by the King.

Addressed from Buckingham Palace and dated 6th February, 1935, it read: 'It was so very kind of you to send me such an inspiring message from my dear mother. I fully understand what she has thought fit to convey to me through your instrumentality. I also thank you for the enclosure, viz, *Psychic News,* which I shall certainly peruse with pleasure.

'My mother is constantly with me, watching and guiding my private affairs.

'I appreciate her message about a dark cloud shadowing the home, but a happy reunion in the land of eternal sunshine.' Less than a year later George V passed on.

A curious spirit message concerning the King once came in unusual circumstances. It also involved Mrs Gordon Moore.

Early in March, 1935, a messenger arrived at Mrs Gordon Moore's home. He told her maid he was commanded to wait for a reply.

Mrs Gordon Moore wrote: 'I opened the note, and to my surprise it was an urgent request to go to a well-known London club to meet a Member of Parliament and his wife, neither of whom I knew, at 11 o'clock the next morning. The note was from a man we had met several times and liked.'

She showed it to her husband and asked if he would accompany her.

The couple set off the following morning. At first they saw no one in the club-room.

Then Mrs Gordon Moore made out 'the figure of a tall, practical-looking woman in country clothes, standing at the side of a heavily curtained window.' She asked if the woman knew Mr Q, the writer of the note.

Looking relieved, she said quickly: 'Oh you must be Mrs Gordon Moore. Mr Q and my husband will be here in a moment.'

The two men arrived as she spoke, apologising for the mysterious summons and expressing their thanks. Though their manner was charming, they appeared to find some difficulty in revealing their mission.

The tall woman's husband began, 'I-er-we heard from Mr Q that you might be able to help us in a rather unusual matter.' He hesitated. Mrs Gordon Moore gently asked in what way she could be of use.

'It may seem very odd,' the man replied, 'but we believe you understand messages from the unseen. You do, don't you?' 'Yes, I do,' she answered. 'Well,' he continued, 'we want someone to give a message and thought perhaps you, understanding these things, could do this for us.'

Mystified, the hearer commented, 'Surely you could do this yourselves much better than I or anyone?'

'No, we want a direct secret message given. It is urgent. Our name must not appear for obvious reasons and we do not want it broadcast. It must be a strictly private message.'

Mrs Gordon Moore asked, 'Who must be told?'

'One of the King's younger sons,' came the surprising response. 'Could you do this?' Mrs Gordon Moore said she did not think it was possible, but asked for the message.

Both the man and his wife looked worried. After a few moments' silence the husband said quietly:

'We trust you. I know we can. This is the message. "The King is going to die very soon. There may be confusion and danger. A younger son will succeed and should be prepared."' Mrs Gordon Moore was astounded. 'Surely the Prince of Wales will succeed when the time comes,' she said. 'No,' she was told. 'He won't succeed. He will disappear and a younger son will reign.'

Mrs Gordon Moore asked how these details were known. The tall woman, she was told, had suddenly become entranced for the first time some weeks earlier. The controlling spirit entity repeated again and again over the next days the same message, until the bemused couple decided to try to find a means of delivering it.

Mrs Gordon Moore knew that if she delivered the message in the King's lifetime, it would cause distress and anxiety to many people. Reluctantly, the couple agreed nothing further should be done.

Similarly, medium Leslie Flint also described an incident concerning George V, in his now out of print book *Voices in the Dark*.

Noting that two sitters had booked in as Mrs Brown and Miss Smith, Leslie felt they could have shown more imagination in their choice of pseudonyms. 'This blatancy made the ladies' suspicions of me very obvious,' he wrote.

'Many sitters made it abundantly clear their only purpose in sitting with me was to find out what trick I employed to produce the voices.'

At this seance one communicator announced himself as Alec Holden. An animated conversation ensued between the communicator and his widow, one of the two women.

He intimated that she and her friend had held unspecified positions of great trust. Then the group heard an elderly man's voice, at first indistinct. When it became clear, the two incognito sitters' spontaneous reaction was to rise and curtsey to their 'dead' monarch.

After the sitting, Mrs Holden revealed she and her friend had been attached for many years to the royal household. The unmistakable voice was that of King George V.

Turning to the Queen, a few years ago it was reported that of the many periodicals to pop through the Royal letterbox was the *Quarterly Review* of the Churches' Fellowship for Psychical and Spiritual Studies. Three years earlier it was claimed that Prince Philip, Prince Charles and Princess Anne had their fortunes told by a local peasant woman when they visited the tiny state of Liechtenstein. The same journalist wrote that their hosts, Prince Franz Josef II and his wife, Princess Gina, were reputedly uncannily accurate fortune-tellers and would tell the fortunes of their Royal guests at a New Year's Eve Party.

What cannot be denied is that for many years the Queen has been a fervent believer in homoeopathy, an alternative form of medicine which even today is frowned upon by many doctors, though it is available on the national health service.

It is also worth noting that psychic healer Kay Kiernan has treated the Queen for an injured shoulder. Also a former nurse, Kay then forty-five, was a qualified therapist. She used a special machine, an American invention, which emits high-frequency radio waves, to ease a sprain that the Queen got while chopping wood.

The machine encouraged the adrenal glands of the liver to remove toxins, produce anti-bodies and release defence cells.

Kay stressed her treatment had no connection 'with my long-distance, thought-healing powers. It is a completely practical way of treating injuries.

'The Queen was very interested and asked me questions about the machine.'

The devise, called diapulse, was also used to treat injured players at Arsenal Football Club.

'It is true I have psychic powers,' said Kay. 'I send healing messages by thought power with an actor friend.

'It is also true to say we have cured some people who were thought to be incurable. But that does not mean I am anything other than a normal person.'

An early patient was Princess Margaret. 'I've known her for twenty years,' said Kay. 'We get on well together. I have been to her home at Kensington Palace as a guest. She is a very sweet and lovely person.

'She tells everybody about my machine. If members of the Palace staff need treatment she sends them here in one of her cars.'

It was Princess Margaret who recommended the Queen to Kay after her shoulder failed to respond to ordinary treatment.

Princess Alexandra, the report claimed, had also been treated by Kay for fibrositis.

'I don't know how this leaked out about my Royal patients,' said Kay, 'but it is true I have treated Princess Alexandra as well.

'I don't discuss my patients' symptoms. I have known Princess Alexandra since she was seventeen.'

Had Kay's psychic powers given any hint that she would treat Royalty?

'I did have a vision one day that I would get great help from some famous people in getting across to the world the machine's qualities,' she replied.

On a lighter note, the Queen and Princess Margaret as children used to enjoy playing charades—at which they were very good—with their friends. When congratulated on her skill, Princess Margaret once replied, 'It's quite easy if Lillibet (the family name for the Queen) and I are doing it because there is a kind of telepathy between us.' And for all we know it still exists.

But to return to where we began, with Harry Edwards. He was promised a royal oak tree from Windsor in recognition of his twenty-five years' healing. At a celebratory dinner, John Findlay, then vice-chairman of the National Federation of Spiritual Healers, told how he had written to the Queen drawing attention to Edwards' twenty-five years of continuous healing. The result was a promise from Buckingham Palace that a Windsor Park ranger would earmark a suitable oak sapling for Edwards' sanctuary grounds. 'We will take great care of the tree and have a seat under it,' said Edwards.

Spirit healers also featured in a modern crisis which struck Royalty within comparatively recent years. None was more dramatic than the row which divided Dutchman against Dutchman, and split the Court. A battle royal erupted after Queen Julianna of the Netherlands did nothing more outrageous than ask a faith healer to help restore her young daughter's sight. Yet the bitter arguments which followed this move rocked the very throne upon which she sat and led to press stories and scandal-mongering tales the world over about Juliana's possible divorce and enforced abdication.

The almost painfully shy Queen, one of Europe's longest-serving monarchs, succeeded in 1948 when her mother, Queen Wilhelmina, abdicated in her favour. Even today the Greet Hofmans affair still causes talk among the Dutch. Yet despite the storm the Hofmans affair caused, three months after the death of Prince Bernhardt's mother it was revealed that he called a healer to her bedside in Warmelo Castle.

The Hofmans healing scandal, which broke in 1956, caused press headlines, the like of which had never been seen before. Queen Juliana, who announced her abdication in 1980, summoned Miss Hofmans to the Dutch royal palace to treat her baby daughter Marijke who was born half blind. The healing, which continued for over five years, did not succeed. But the fact that Miss Hofmans treated the Princess aroused unprecedented antagonism among the Dutch government ministers.

It was also said to cause a rift between the Queen and her husband to the extent that the possibility of a divorce was mentioned. Newspapers tagged the healer a female Rasputin. At one stage it was even suggested Juliana should abdicate. Another claim was that the healer was hypnotising the monarch. An anonymous close friend of Prince

Bernhardt said: 'When we went to Paris, Jula was herself again. Our talk became free and intimate. None of the Hofmans' messages from God were mentioned.' But back in Holland 'it started all over again.' It was even said that Eleanor Roosevelt was called in by Bernhardt to 'make Jula see.' But to no avail.

Some months after the crisis, it was announced that three prominent members of the Royal household had been dismissed. These were Baron van Heeckeren van Molecanten, head of the secretariat, Dr van Maasdijk, a chamberlain, and Miss M. de Jong, the Queen's private secretary. All three were regarded as persons trying to influence the Queen into continuing her association with Miss Hofmans.

A few weeks earlier the Cabinet issued a statement over the matter. This was a reply to Dr J. W. Beyen, former Foreign Minister. The attacks came from Dr van Maasdijk, one of the Queen's gentlemen-in-waiting, who accused Dr Beyen of bungling the Hofmans affair by confirming 'difficulties' at the palace at a meeting of Dutch editors. The statement said, 'Like the whole Cabinet, Dr Beyen has done everything to protect Juliana against unjust attacks.'

Miss Hofmans—she died in 1968 at the age of seventy-three—enraged the political scene. After a general election politicians refused to form a government until the healer was banished. She was. But twice the healer was renounced.

The first renouncement came after a three-man committee met. Set up by the Queen and her husband, its brief was to investigate the circumstances which led to reports of a rift between them. Queen Juliana, it was announced, would no longer attend religious conferences in which the healer was said to play a leading part at the home of the Queen's mother. Miss Hofmans would be left free to do what she wanted; the committee did not know her present whereabouts. Reports indicated that the court was split into two factions, for and against the healer, whose influence was said to be one reason for the alleged Royal marriage rift.

'I will not leave my patients,' said the healer when told about the announcement. 'I will not leave this country. I will hold my prayer meetings as usual.' She described the official communiqué as 'a mixture of conflicting and untrue statements,' adding: 'The truth will emerge in the long run. I am in the hands of the Lord.'

At the height of the crisis, then Prime Minister Dr Drees, categorically denied that Juliana had caused a constitutional crisis through her association with Miss Hofmans. Asked at a press conference if the healer had any influence over the monarch he replied: 'I do not know. All I can say is that the Queen has at all times acted constitutionally.'

He was also asked if Miss Hofmans could be prosecuted for healing, whether she took money or not. He answered in the affirmative, adding: 'This woman is only praying. She prescribes no medicine. Is there any country in which one can be punished for praying for someone?' Miss Hofmans' activities had been fully investigated and were within the law. Earlier Lord Dowding, an avowed Spiritualist who masterminded the Battle of Britain, told a public meeting: I know Miss Hofmans. She is a completely selfless, dedicated woman.'

At that time J. W. Kasier, describing himself as a 'kindred spirit of Miss Hofmans,' issued a statement by her. It was the first public comment made by Miss Hofmans.

'My work exists only by dedicating man to Christ for all needs of human meaning,' it stated. The announcement denied that the healer had never interfered with the individual freedom of any patient, and that applied to Juliana. The healer added: 'The effectiveness of the help is not in my hands. The realisation of the help is individual so that no fixed rule can be given.

'It goes without saying that individual freedom is not interfered with so that the progress of the help for the healing is in the hands of the person concerned. It is my task to transmit the appropriate inspiration or the healing process to everybody during innumerable personal contacts and also by letter and telephone. These inspirations are in the fields of man's religious ties and his receptivity for help. This explains my work from beginning to end.'

Despite an announcement that Juliana had severed all links with the healer, two weeks later it was rumoured this was not so. Baron Jakob van Heeckeren confirmed to a British journalist that the link stood. The Baron said 'no doubt' the Queen had resumed her contacts with the healer in her daughter's interests. He had just left a three-hour conference with the monarch.

When a journalist asked Dr G. Lammers, head of the Dutch government's information, 'Will the Queen now repeal her pledge in a public statment?' his reply was 'Emphatically, no.' Moreover, it was said that Miss Hofmans was safely installed in her home, a mere five minutes' bicycle ride from the palace.

Another British journalist claimed that a week after making her break with the healer the Queen was pleading for spiritual help from her former associates. 'I was present at the secret conclave when contact was resumed,' he wrote. It was a conference by Het Oude Loo, an organisation in which Miss Hofmans was a leading figure. The meeting was held in the Dutch Royal Palace at Appeldoorn. A leading Dutch delegate explained the Queen would not attend in case it caused a new storm of protests. But a tape recording of every word spoken was said to be rushed to the monarch each night as soon as the day's events were over.

When the healer resumed her work in Amsterdam, over 700 patients consulted her, three times as many as before the crisis. Her consulting room was in a dancing school over a cafe. Her home, a converted railway coach, was in the grounds of a wealthy insurance company director. His wife told a reporter that Miss Hofmans' plans were to continue her work as usual.

During the crisis Miss Hofmans visited Britain to attend a conference in Margate, Kent, of the International Centre for Spiritual Studies. At that time the old *Sunday Pictorial* told of a 'sensational disclosure.' This was a plot to dethrone Juliana in favour of Princess Beatrix. An interview was arranged with Dr van Maasdijk.

He denied that three statesmen had extracted any promise from Juliana to break off her relationship with Miss Hofmans. 'It is inconceivable,' he said, 'as it would be in England. The Queen,' he added, 'has promised to stop seeing the healer for the time being if her relationship with Miss Hofmans was an obstacle to solving the crisis. The Queen has kept her word absolutely. Greet Hofmans has not been to the palace for three-and-a-half years, although the Queen has been to see her. Today Miss Hofmans never touches the young Princess Marijke. She merely prays for her a few minutes each day.'

The reporter was told that those plotting the Queen's downfall were trying to enlist the help of Bernhardt's mother, the Princess Armgard Lippe—Biesterfeld. When he rang the Queen's private secretary to thank him for arranging the meeting with van Maasdijk, he said: 'What you have heard is the truth. Tell it to your people.' After reading the report the Princess said she could not—or would not?—comment.

However, an anonymous 'friend' of Prince Bernhardt said the healer was installed in a room at the palace; the Queen had long conversations with her. Bernhardt disapproved of their friendship, though he had introduced them. He felt his wife was 'withdrawing from reality' by her religious preoccupation. The Prince did not interest himself in the conferences held at the Royal Palace at Apeldoorn.

According to his friend, Bernhardt 'always had pressing business elsewhere. What went on was reported back to the Palace as talk of world peace through mysticism and moral rearmament. It did not make a great deal of sense. But it was clear to all that she and Bernhardt were living almost apart. All he could do until Juliana "came to her senses," as he put it, was to keep up pretences.'

Miss Hofmans, a former secretary, said her healing began after 'a voice started to speak to me. The voice told me I had a mission to fulfil. At first I thought I was dreaming, but the voice came back again. It was the voice of God telling me that I was to act as a medium between him and suffering humanity. He gave me instructions, definite formulas on how to heal.'

Despite his antagonism towards Miss Hofmans, it was revealed in 1971 that Prince Bernhardt approached famous Dutch healer and psychic detective Gerard Croiset, seeking help for his mother. He sent his son to the Princess, then in her eighties.

Altogether Croiset junior made nine visits. Before her death the Princess, who died of cancer, endured terrible pain. His visits were admitted by the court. However, Dutch Government spokesmen denied that the healer also forecast the specific time of her death and that Bernhardt rushed back from America on his authority.

But perhaps the much-maligned Greet Hofmans should have the last word. 'I receive messages from above,' she said. 'But I do not hear a voice. It is just a certainty that what I am going to say is right. I do not call myself a healer. I may, by intuition, advise a sick person so that he becomes well again.'

Four years later, however, the King of Nepal consulted a medium with, as far as one can tell, no public outcry or society scandal. Just over a month after his sitting with leading British medium Norah Blackwood, King Mahendra assumed full powers in his Himalayan kingdom, which lay between India and Tibet.

The King, then thirty-nine, came to Britain during a State visit. On his return, with 'sensational suddenness' he arrested the socialist Prime Minister B. P. Koirala and desolved the government. Lawlessness, said the monarch, had increased and 'anti-national elements' encouraged. The situation could not be left to continue 'in the guise of democracy.' He added, 'I am taking these steps because it is my ultimate responsibility to maintain the order, integrity and sovereignty of the country.'

While he was in Britain an attempt was made to overthrow the government. Seven people died when police opened fire on a mob said to be inspired by a band of 'reactionary elements posing as Hindu mystic yogis.' It was about this time that the King was welcomed to the Belgravia headquarters of the Spiritualist Association of Great Britain by the then president Eric Stuart, who had been invited to a reception given by the Nepal Embassy a few days previously.

Mrs Blackwood, respecting the King's wish that the seance's contents be kept strictly private, would not comment. King Mahendra insisted on sitting completely alone with the medium. Diplomats, officers of his own staff and Spiritualist Association officials were excluded from the room. After the seance, the King commented that it was 'very satisfactory.' Eric Stuart too refused to be drawn, apart from saying that Mrs Blackwood was one of the Association's principal mediums, and that the monarch was 'most interested in our work.' But, he added, 'the ethics of our Association will not allow me to discuss the sittings.'

Turning to Greece—and remember that Prince Philip has family connections with that country—there is proof that more than one Greek King sat with mediums.

When King George II of Greece died in 1947 it was revealed that he sat regularly with a London medium, Estelle Roberts. Even when the King died, Mrs Roberts refused to give details of their seances. She had not been given his permission so to do: the fact that he had died did not release her from obligations of secrecy. However, Mrs Roberts did say, 'During the many years that I knew King George, he never once asked me about his health, although he knew my psychic powers enabled me to diagnose illness.' The medium made this comment in the monarch's defence after one paper claimed he was a hypochondriac who 'ran after quack doctors.'

On numerous occasions the King was to be seen at Mrs Roberts' public demonstrations of clairvoyance in Central London. He also attended speeches by Spiritualist author Shaw Desmond, and was present at the opening of the House of Red Cloud, named after the medium's North American spirit guide.

The King did not appear to be attracted by physical seance-room phenomena. Rather he was satisfied with trance manifestations and clairvoyant messages. A great-grandson of Queen Victoria, the King came from a family sympathetic to matters psychic. His uncle, Prince Christophere of Greece, told in his memoires how a medium predicted much of the dark future of the family through wars, revolt and exile.

He wrote: 'The night before my father died, my brother Constantine and I had an experience which we could never explain. A lady attached to the Red Cross in Janina was very much interested in Spiritualism and persuaded us to take part in an experiment in automatic writing that evening . . . For a few minutes it (the pencil) flew over the paper so quickly that we could hardly keep our fingers on it. Then it stopped as abruptly as it had begun. The message was for Constantine. It promised him fame and glory, the winning of two wars and after that much sorrow. But below was written the word "Death" several times and then "Tomorrow." The rest was illegible. The next day Father was assassinated.' It is a matter of history that Constantine—King George's father—did become King of Greece, won two Balkan wars and was afterwards deposed. And he did suffer much sorrow.

After George's death comment came from Captain C. M. Melas, CBE, of the Greek Royal Navy. 'Of course King George was a Spiritualist,' he said. 'And he did not care who knew it. His tremendous faith in the spirit world helped him to bear his heavy cross during the difficult years of the war. In that faith he gave his famous "No!" to Mussolini in 1940 knowing that the independent spirit of his country would in the end prevail.

'He had been told from Beyond that the sacrifice his country had made would not be in vain. It was a common thing for the spirit of King George's father to communicate messages for his son . . . A few days before Prince Christophere fell ill and passed away I had seen him, and as he was a powerful medium, I had asked him if he would kindly sit with us. He promised to do so.

'His spirit came in the dark days of the Italian invasion to give us courage. It was a fortnight after the Italian attack and the Italian army was near my home town of Janina when Prince Christophere came through and brought us the conviction of victory. It was from these spirit messages that we drew our faith and in them lay the very essence of King George's Spiritualism.'

King Paul of the Hellenes, who died in 1964, also sat with Estelle Roberts. He came to Britain with his brother, King George, who was

deposed when Greece was proclaimed a republic in 1924. Red C
foretold that King George would return to the throne, an event w
occurred in 1935, although the prediction was received with sceptic.
In the ensuing eleven years until the King's 1947 death there was a
stream of letters between monarch and medium. Red Cloud dictated
the answers to Mrs Roberts, which were sent to the sovereign in the
official diplomatic bag. When George died Paul succeeded him to the
throne. After his introduction to Mrs Roberts by his brother, Paul sat
privately with the medium at least a dozen times.

King Paul, a cousin of Prince Philip, used the name Mr Constantine
whenever he visited Estelle. And after her death in 1981 it was revealed
that ex-Queen Frederika of Greece, Paul's wife, sat with veteran
medium Bertha Harris. Her forecast, fulfilled many years later, was that
her son Constantine would become King, lose his throne and end by
living as an English gentleman.

Finally, two other Queens have also consulted a Greek medium, Dr
Filo Karakassi, a gynaecologist of Athens. Queen Anne-Marie of Greece
sent a request through a court official. She was advised during her
pregnancy to have a Caesarian birth. The question she asked was
whether to accept the advice. 'You must wait,' said the medium. 'Then
you will have a natural birth of a girl.' Anne-Marie accepted Filo's
counsel. After the medium proved to be right about the natural birth
and arrival of a daughter she sent a letter of gratitude and congratulation
on her accuracy.

The medium's fame even spread to what was then known as Persia.
An official made the long journey with a similar request from Queen
Farah. Should she have the Caesarian birth advocated by medical
advisers? Again the medium's answer was 'No.' She advised a natural
birth, stating that a boy would be born. The official Royal letter of
gratitude which, like Anne-Marie's hung in the medium's home,
specified how glad the Queen was that Filo was right in announcing the
birth of a baby boy.

Now, Farah has been driven from her home, a refugee from her own
kingdom, her husband dead. I do not know if he has returned in some
far off seance room. One day he may break the barrier between two
worlds. Then, like other monarchs before him, he too will prove that
dead King's can speak.

Winston Wins Through

IN ITS LONG and chequered history, Britain has produced some of the finest statesmen the world has ever known, or will ever know. Their impact on global affairs cannot be measured. No one would deny that vital, inspiring role Winston Churchill played in the dark, seemingly endless days of the Second World War. Underarmed and underfire, Britain struggled through, defying the enemy forces which, after the invasion of Europe by Germany, were a mere few miles away across the English Channel.

Churchill's speeches to the nation are legendary and will remain so. His slow, measured tones stirred the country to action. He was a rallying point, epitomising the fighting spirit of ordinary folk not only in Britain but throughout the Free World and Commonwealth. Few know, however, that it was a hunch during the Boer War that probably saved Churchill's life. In fact, psychic incidents peppered the Premier's career and once warned him about a Downing Street bomb attack. But for a premonition kitchen staff at No 10 would have been killed, and just think what mileage the enemy propaganda machine would have got out of that.

Winston was born in 1874 at the family mansion, Blenheim Palace. His father, Lord Randolph Churchill, was a leading politician of the time and one of the sons of the Seventh Duke of Marlborough. As a child Winston was not particularly bright. Though he did not distinguish himself at his lessons, the future world leader began to show brilliance at English, a brilliance which was to inspire millions of men and women as they literally did battle with Nazi forces.

His education complete, the young Churchill obtained a job as a war correspondent for the *Morning Post* and in October 1899 set sail for South Africa. At the Cape, Churchill caught the last train that would enable him to take a short cut to the front in Natal. This meant he would gain several days on other war correspondents in the area.

Within a month of arriving the armoured train on which Churchill was a passenger was ambushed by the dreaded Boers. Literally rolling up his sleeves, Churchill was successful in freeing the carriage that blocked the line. But there was a price to pay. Churchill was captured and taken to a prisoner of war camp at Pretoria. Not for long, though. By vaulting over a wall, Churchill escaped. With only chocolate to nourish him, the future Premier found the railway line, jumped on a train and alighted at Witbank, which was totally unknown territory to him.

Utterly alone not knowing where to seek help or if he might be betrayed to enemy authorities Winston 'realised with awful force that no exercise of my own feeble wit and strength could save me from my enemies. Without the assistance of that High Power which interferes in the eternal sequence of cause and effect more often than we are always prone to admit, I could never succeed.'

Churchill prayed for help and guidance. He later recalled: 'My prayer, as it seemed to me, was simply and wonderfully answered. Suddenly, without the slightest reason, all my doubts disappeared. It was certainly by no process of logic they were dispelled. I just felt quite clear I would go to the Kaffir kraal.'

For several hours Churchill had pondered the advisability of making for the village he could see in the distance. In former years he had sometimes held a pencil 'and written while others had touched my wrist or hand. I acted in exactly the same unconscious manner now.'

Churchill walked towards a fire he could see in the distance and approached a group of houses around the mouth of a coalmine. Close by he noticed a small yet substantial stone house. The young correspondent stood and thought. What should he do? Ought he to seek help at one of the houses? After all, he recalled hearing that a number of British residents had been allowed to stay in order to keep the mines working. He wondered if some unseen force had led him to one of these.

'The odds were heavily against me,' he wrote later. 'It was with faltering and reluctant steps that I walked out of the shimmering gloom of the veldt into the light of the furnace fires, advanced towards the silent house, and struck with my fist upon the door.' After a pause and with his heart thumping away Churchill knocked a second time. A light shone upstairs: a window opened. 'Wer ist da?' asked a male voice. 'I felt the shock of disappointment and consternation to my fingers,' Churchill wrote in his autobiography. He asked the stranger for help, using the excuse he had suffered an accident.

Next came footsteps down the stairs. The young escapee listened as a bolt was drawn back and the lock turned. The door opened abruptly. In the darkness Churchill saw in a passage a tall man with a dark moustache. 'What do you want?' the stranger demanded . . . in English. 'I am a burgher,' said Churchill. 'I have had an accident. I was going to join my commander at Komati Port. I have fallen off the train. I think I have dislocated my shoulder.' The stranger looked at Churchill suspiciously. 'Well,' he said at last, 'come in.'

Young Winston entered, wondering if the house would be his prison. The man lit a lamp and set it on the table. Deliberating for a while, he continued, 'I think I would like to know a little more about this railway accident of yours.'

Winston hesitated. Plucking up his courage he replied, 'I think I had better tell you the truth.' 'I think you had,' came the reply. It was then Churchill took the plunge, gave his name, and admitted he was a war correspondent, and for a British paper. 'I escaped last night from Pretoria,' he confessed. 'I am making my way to the frontier. I have plenty of money. Will you help me?'

There was another long, seemingly unending pause. Then the man rose from the table and locked the door. The stranger advanced towards Winston, holding out his hand. 'Thank God you have come here,' he cried. 'It is the only house for twenty miles where you would not have been handed over. But we are all British here. We will see you through.'

Recalling the incident Churchill recorded: 'It is easier to recall across the gulf of years the spasm of relief which swept over me than it is to describe it. A moment before I had thought myself trapped; and now friends, food, resources, aid were all at my disposal. I felt like a drowning man pulled out of the water and informed he had won the Derby.'

The man, Churchill learned, was an English manager of Transvaal Collieries. He hid Winston in the mine, then secreted among bales of wool on a train, the young correspondent made his way to Portuguese East Africa and took a steamer to Durban where he continued to report the war. Subsequently Churchill learned that a reward had been offered for his capture. The notice read: '£25 sterling reward is offered by the sub-commission of the fifth division, on behalf of the Special Constable of the said division, to anyone who brings the escaped prisoner of war, Churchill, dead or alive.'

That was one of just several well-documented psychic happenings in Churchill's life. One example speedily springs to mind. In the early days of the First World War Churchill resigned his Parliamentary seat to fight on the Western Front. One day he was summoned to see the General. While he was there, his crude dugout was blown to pieces.

'And then,' Churchill said later, 'there came the sensation that a hand had been stretched out to move me in the nick of time from a fatal spot.' Writing to his wife from the trenches he stated: 'Believe me, I am superior to anything that can happen to me out here. My conviction that the greatest of my work is still to be done is strong within me and I ride reposefully along the gale.' How right he was.

Though no one will deny that one of Churchill's finest aspects were his speeches, Baroness Asquith once revealed that in his early political days he was unable to say more than a sentence in reply in the House of Commons unless he had written it out beforehand and committed it to memory. Churchill always tried to foresee the situations that would present themselves and prepare several variants ready to meet any possibility. The Baroness said he did not deviate from this practice throughout his long and distinguished parliamentary career. 'By some sixth sense,' she wrote, 'he was able to foresee the bull's-eye before it was presented. It was largely to this gift of inspired and accurate prevision that he owed his mastery of debate.'

Some years ago the Baroness revealed that every prophecy Churchill made in the 1930s was fulfilled. In 1925 he foretold the coming of the H-bomb, radar, the V1 and V2 German missiles.

'May there not be methods of using explosive energy more intense than anything yet discovered?' Churchill mused. 'Might not a bomb no bigger than an orange be found to possess a secret power to . . . concentrate the force of a thousand tons of cordite? Could not explosives . . . be guided automatically in flying machines by wireless or other rays, without a human pilot?'

When Britain declared war on Germany in the dark days of 1939 Neville Chamberlain was then Prime Minister. Churchill sat on the front bench and listened to the grim pronouncements of his fellow MPs. After hearing the first of many dreaded air-raid sirens he said: 'I felt a serenity of mind and was conscious of a kind of uplifted detachment from human and personal affairs. The glory of Old England, peace-loving and ill-prepared as she was, but instant and fearless at the call of honour, thrilled my being and seemed to lift our fate to those spheres far removed from earthly facts and physical sensation.'

Not surprisingly, Churchill was offered a seat in the war Cabinet as First Lord of the Admiralty. In May 1940 Hitler invaded Holland and Belgium. MPs met to censure the Government's handling of the war. The Labour Party made it clear it would not serve under Chamberlain. The Prime Minister, Churchill and Lord Halifax then discussed the selection of the nation's next leader. Churchill was selected. 'I felt,' he said, 'as if I were walking with Destiny, and that all my past life had been but a preparation for this hour and for this trial.'

In his broadcast to the nation in 1940 the new Premier referred to Britain's 'physical energy and psychic strength.' Discussing war losses two years later he said, 'Only faith in a life after death, in a brighter world, where dear ones will meet again—only that and the measured tramp of time can give consolation.'

Three years later Churchill when addressing miners stated in his characteristic tones: 'I sometimes have a feeling—in fact, I have it very strongly—a feeling of interference. I want to stress it. I have a feeling sometimes that some guiding hand has interfered. I have a feeling that we have a Guardian because we serve a great cause and that we shall have that Guardian as long as we serve that cause faithfully.'

In that same year, War Cabinet members spoke secretly to 6,000 women at London's famous Albert Hall. Churchill expressed the hope that in the post-war world 'the name of our dear country will, by our conduct, by our clairvoyance . . . long stand in honour among nations of the world. I have no fear of the future. Let us go forward with its mysteries, let us tear aside the veils which hide it from our eyes.'

To return to the war years, Churchill was outraged when a medium was brought to London to face trial at the Old Bailey. This concerned a materialisation medium, Helen Duncan, in whose presence the dead literally appeared, walked and talked.

Mrs Duncan was arrested after one of her seances was raided in Portsmouth, Hants. She was charged under the Witchcraft Act. Though beleaguered with war-time problems, Churchill wrote a note to the Home Secretary. It demanded: 'Let me have a report on the Witchcraft Act of 1735. What was the cost of a trial to the State in which the Recorder was kept busy with all this obsolete tomfoolery to the detriment of the necessary work in the courts?'

Probably known to Churchill, one of Britain's other Allies was led by a convinced and avowed Spiritualist, Canadian Premier Mackenzie King. Medium Lilian Bailey, well known within Spiritualist circles, gave King several sittings. During the war he once telephoned her saying he was ill and unable to keep his appointment. Could she visit his Dorchester Hotel suite? Mrs Bailey did as requested. Shown into King's bedroom, she noticed Churchill. As he rose to leave, Churchill grinned at her. 'You be careful, my girl,' he joked to Mrs Bailey, 'or you may find yourself in the Tower of London.'

During the war years Churchill risked life and limb by making frequent tours at night of anti-aircraft gun sites during the Blitz. Everyone was appalled by his disregard of danger. His wife, Clementine, thought of a solution. She requested that an armoured car be placed at his disposal. When the chauffeur remarked that Mr Churchill would not ride in such a vehicle, she replied that he would be forced to if no other car were waiting for him.

The first time Churchill saw the car outside No 10 he asked, 'What is this for?' He would not ride in the new vehicle, he asserted, but in a police car. This was not available, the Premier was told. Mrs Churchill had taken quiet steps to have it withdrawn. Furious at being baulked, Churchill climbed into the offending vehicle and was driven off.

As they travelled, the car was peppered with shrapnel, which smashed the bonnet. Bombs narrowly missed the car.

At Richmond Park the Prime Minister alighted to watch the gun crews in action. As he was about to leave, he walked up to one of the staff drivers and queried, 'Is this car armoured?' Told it was not, Churchill immediately commandeered one of the ordinary staff cars for his return journey. As usual, the nearside door was opened for him. He always sat that side.

For no apparent reason Churchill paused, turned, opened the far door himself and sat down. He had never done this before.

As they travelled along the Kingston by-pass, Surrey, at 60mph, a bomb dropped close to the car. So violent was the explosion that two wheels were lifted from the ground. It almost overturned, but at the last moment righted itself.

'That was a near one,' Churchill commented. 'It must have been my beef at this side that pulled it down.' If he had been sitting in his usual seat, the car would have overturned. Though he did not tell his wife,

Clementine learned of the incident and asked him why he had sat on the far side.

'I don't know,' he replied at first. Then he added: 'Of course I know. Something said to me "Stop" before I reached the car door held open for me. It then appeared to me I was told I was meant to open the door on the other side and get in and sit there—and that's what I did.'

Churchill's 'fortunate inspiration' which undoubtedly saved the lives of several Downing Street kitchen staff happened one autumn evening in October 1940 when the Prime Minister was dining at home. Suddenly the all too frequent wail of sirens echoed through London's bombed, defiant streets. Immediately, using some psychic sense Churchill became aware that something unpleasant was about to happen. A picture flashed into his mind. Bombs were falling on Horse Guards Parade, which backed on to the house. Realising that the twenty-five feet high plate glass window of No 10's kitchen had no substantial protection against glass and splinters, Churchill hastened to tell the butler to put dinner on the hotplate and usher the staff to the shelter.

He then returned to his place at the table. Three minutes later he heard a crash, and a violent shock.

The Premier's detective hurried in with the message that a great deal of damage had been done to the kitchen, pantry and offices. Churchill recorded in his diary:

'We went into the kitchen to view the scene. The devastation was complete. The blast had smitten the large, tidy kitchen, with all its bright saucepans and crockery, into a heap of black dust and rubble. The big plate-glass window had been hurled in fragments and splinters across the room, and would, of course, have cut its occupants, if there had been any, to pieces. But my fortunate inspiration, which I might so easily have neglected, had come in the nick of time.'

After the magnificent, inspiring—and inspired—shepherding of Britain through the worst that Hitler's mighty armies, navy and the Luftwaffe could perpetrate, Winston Churchill reaped a sorry reward.

He tried to have the general election postponed, but it was forced upon him in 1945, before the defeat of Japan.

The night before the election, he revealed in his war memoirs, he went to bed in the belief that the British people would wish him to continue his work. Churchill recorded: 'Just before dawn I woke suddenly with a sharp stab of almost physical pain. A hitherto subconscious conviction that we were beaten broke forth and dominated my mind.

'All the pressure of great events, on and against which I had mentally so long maintained my "flying speed," would cease, and I should fall. The power to shape the future would be denied me.

'The knowledge and experience I had gathered, the authority and goodwill I had gained in so many countries, would vanish. I was discontented at the prospect and turned over at once to sleep again.'

A few hours later, after the votes had been counted, Winston Churchill, who had borne on his capable shoulders such a heavy burden for five long years, laid it down in handing his resignation to the King.

As a post script it is worth adding that had Churchill followed a seer's advice, Britain's post war government would have been radically changed if the statesman had listened to a famous psychic. Churchill met internationally known American clairvoyant Jeane Dixon at a party given in his honour in 1945 by Lord Halifax, then Britain's Ambassador to the United States. 'Mr Prime Minister,' the Washington psychic pleaded, 'please don't call an early election or you will be defeated.' Churchill's grunted reply, 'England will never let me down,' was soon proved to be incorrect.

Journalist Hannen Swaffer, the 'Pope of Fleet Street,' an expert on Spiritualism and mediumship, was totally convinced Churchill had psychic gifts.

Writing of him a year after hostilities ceased, Swaffer commented: 'I have known Winston for over thirty years. Before the war he was just a leading politician. In 1940 and 1941 he became an inspired leader of nations, one of the outstanding men of history . . .

'I believe that during those fateful years there stood behind him Hampden and Cromwell and Pitt—and all those great upholders of liberty with whom our nation has been blessed. We know from his autobiography that Winston has psychic gifts. They stood him in good stead when his need was greatest.'

Did Churchill himself ever sit with a medium like his counterpart Mackenzie King? Though there is no independent documentary evidence, before she died veteran clairvoyant Bertha Harris claimed that he did.

Bertha, who lived in Golders Green, NW London, maintained that at the height of her fame during the war she met Churchill and General de Gaulle, who was then living in exile.

'Churchill was very mediumistic,' said Bertha. 'I think he was often guided by those Beyond. He would take five-minute naps when he was worried and wake, completely refreshed, knowing exactly what to do.' In Bertha's view in reality they were not naps, but a kind of trance.

Further evidence of Churchill's afterlife acceptance was gained by Alderman T. J. Brooks, MP. Recollecting his first day at the House of Commons, Brooks stated: 'I had a thrill. Churchill, moving a resolution on the death of the Duke of Kent, said, "He has gone to join a happy family." How did he know? I saw Churchill afterwards and told him, "I was thrilled by your words.'

'"Oh, why was that?" he asked. I repeated his sentence and said, "Do you believe that?"

'He replied, "I do." 'I asked. "Is it true then?" He answered, "There is no doubt about it in my mind."'

Churchill publicly threw his belief behind an afterlife time and time again. 'Most people,' he once stated, 'are going to be very surprised when they go to heaven. They are looking forward to meeting fascinating people like Napoleon and Julius Caesar.

'But they'll probably never even be able to find them, because there will be so many millions of other people there too—Indians and Chinese and people like that. Everyone will have equal rights in heaven. That will be the real Welfare State.' Though a very talented artist, he commented, 'When I get to heaven I would want to spend the first million years painting so that I could get to the depths of it.'

Talking to an American journalist about aerial warfare, Churchill remarked: 'I wonder what God thinks of things his creatures have invented. Really, it's surprising he has allowed it, but then I suppose he has so many things to think of, not only us but all his worlds. I wouldn't have his job for anything. Mine is hard enough, but his is much more difficult. And he can't even resign.'

In the early years of his marriage, he wrote a letter to his beloved Clementine which was to be handed to her in the event of his death. With the detailed financial advice came these words: 'Do not grieve for me too much. I am a spirit confident of my rights. Death is only an incident and not the most important which happens to us in this state of being.'

Moreover, Churchill enjoyed his own funeral service, according to Mary Rogers, a spiritual healer and wife of George Rogers, the former MP for London's Kensington North constituency.

Mrs Rogers, a medium in her own right, claimed she had been in touch with various famous politicians all of whom had one thing in common, despite their political differences. All were dead. These included Walpole, Disraeli, Gladstone, Keir Hardie, Baldwin and Churchill.

The latter, she claimed, 'thoroughly approved of his funeral. He thought it very right and proper and enjoyed every minute of it.' Churchill, she continued, said he liked Harold Wilson and considered him a good man.

Unlike Churchill, many of Britain's Prime Ministers have passed into obscurity. Dead and literally forgotten their names, once so well known, now mean little or nothing to the average person. Some stand head and shoulders above their colleagues. If a role call of famous Premiers were ever called the name of William Ewart Gladstone would certainly figure prominently.

Even today the Grand Old Man is remembered with affection and respect by generations that never knew him. Queen Victoria may well have lamented that he 'speaks to me as if I was a public meeting,' but Gladstone, four time Britain's Premier, still engenders feelings of admiration with many a heart.

But what history books and political works do not record is that while he was Prime Minister, the Liberal Party's most famed advocate had a sitting with William Eglington, a psychic celebrity of his day.

Gladstone considered psychical research to be 'the most important work which is being done in the world—by far the most important.'

Before his sitting with Eglington, which took place in a house in Grosvenor Square, London, Gladstone discussed his attitude to Spiritualism and, according to Eglington, said he was 'already convinced that there were subtle forces with which our puny minds could not deal and which he could not comprehend.'

The statesman also added, said the medium, that he held 'the attitude, therefore, not of a scoffer, but of a student who had no reason to doubt the genuineness of my pretensions.'

Besides Eglington and Gladstone, there were three other sitters. One of them brought two ordinary school slates, while the medium had his own locked double slate. Describing the seance afterwards, Eglington said:

'We began by asking Mr Gladstone to write a question upon one of the school slates. He did so and the slate was held by me beneath the table with the question upon the under side so that I could not see it, the other side being pressed closely against the under side of the table. Presently the writing began.'

Asked whether Gladstone himself heard the spirit communicators writing, the medium went on: 'He did—and his face was a study. His intense look of amazement would have been amusing to those who have had experience of such phenomena, and was intensified when the slate was brought up and the few words which had been written were declared by him to be a pertinent reply to his question.

'The reply was, "In the year 1857," and on the slate being turned over, it was found that his question had been, "Which year do you remember to have been more dry than the present one?"

'After that, Mr Gladstone took the locked slate into a corner of the room, and on the inside of it wrote a question, which of course none of us saw. Then, locking the slate and retaining the key, the slate was handed to one of the ladies and myself, and we both held it in the sight of all.

'While in this position, the writing was heard going on upon the closed surfaces, and upon the slate being opened it was found that the question asked was, "Is the Pope ill or well?" which had been answered in red pencil by the words, "He is ill in mind, not in body."

'Of the subsequent experiments I can only say that they were perfectly successful; that some of the communications were written upon Mrs O's own slates when held under the table; that several messages were given, not only between these two slates, but also within the locked slate, in view of all present; and that some of the questions were put in Spanish, French and Greek, and satisfactorily answered in the same languages.'

Eglington said that he knew a little French, but no Spanish or Greek. He continued: 'The written questions were in every case unknown to me; and pertinent answers, as I have told you, were written between slates fully exposed to view upon, or held over the table of a brilliantly lighted drawing-room, the writing being distinctly heard while in the actual process.

'Mr Gladstone had the fullest opportunity of observation, and I have no doubt whatever that his keen, penetrating eyes, as he carefully watched all that was passing, assured him that everything was genuine.

'As one indication I may mention the evident interest he took in the messages themselves, which he could scarcely have done if he had any suspicion whatever of the bona fides of the experiments. From first to last he made a careful record of all the questions and all the replies.'

Many national newspapers reprinted Eglington's story of the seance from *Light*, a Spiritualist journal, where it first appeared. And the medium's version was never contradicted by Gladstone, who later joined the Society for Psychical Research.

After the seance Gladstone was quoted as saying, doubtless referring to those scientists who opposed psychic research without personal inquiry: 'I have always thought that scientific men run too much in a groove. They do noble work in their own special line of research, but they are too often indisposed to give any attention to matters which seem to conflict with their established modes of thought.

'Indeed they not infrequently attempt to deny that into which they have never inquired, not sufficiently realising the fact that there may possibly be forces in Nature of which they know nothing.'

Though in Britain's history only one Premier has ever been assassinated, ten days before the murderous attack on Spencer Perceval in the lobby of the House of Commons, a Cornish man 'saw' it all.

In 1812 John Williams of Scorrier House, near Redruth, had three successive dreams. Each time he dreamt he was in the lobby of the House. He saw 'a person in a snuff-coloured coat with yellow metal buttons' draw a pistol and shoot a 'small man in a blue coat and white waistcoat.' The victim, Williams was told in his dream, was the Prime Minister. He previewed the murderer being seized and hustled away.

Not unnaturally Williams wanted to go to London to warn Perceval, but was dissuaded from doing so by his incredulous wife and friends. On May 12 the deadly shot was fired. The assassin, a mad bankrupt called Bellingham, was dressed exactly as Williams described in his dreams.

Of modern political leaders, luckily for Harold Wilson a prediction concerning his untimely death was proved totally wrong. In 1969 a Cheshire clairvoyant wrote to the Prime Minister urging extra precautions, especially if he visited the East Coast early the next year.

The seer said he 'saw' a 'rally and Mr Wilson climbing up some steps onto a platform. There appeared to be a strong wind. He was pushing back his hair. Suddenly, he disappeared from view. There was pandemonium as people crowded round.' The psychic thought the assassination attempt would come in March and arise from ill-feeling from the situations regarding what was Rhodesia and Nigeria. Luckily for Harold Wilson, the attempt was never made.

Sir Harold, as he later became, is Britain's longest-serving peacetime Prime Minister this century. Intriguingly, once he was asked in an interview to consider 'a gathering of his predecessors in the hypothetical hereafter.'

The statesman added he would find Pitt interesting, 'but I do not know what the facilities are like in the hereafter . . . I think he would be getting up all the time saying he had important papers to read.' What's more rumour has it that one of Sir Harold's favourite after-dinner recreations is turning out the lights and telling ghost stories—with a Parliamentary setting, naturally.

Meanwhile, probably unbeknown to him, Sir Harold was mentioned during one of Hugh Gaitskell's alleged spirit returns. It occurred in 1963, a few months after the Labour leader's death. A statement signed by twenty-five people stated that Gaitskell was recognised when he superimposed his facial features at a seance with medium Frank Christmas.

He returned, they claimed, to speak to Eva Sherriff, a London medium who waited at tables in the members' restaurant at the House of Commons. Gaitskell mentioned people who had met him after passing on. So what was his message? Gaitskell, the sitters explained, said he was not displeased that his friend Harold Wilson had been chosen to succeed him as leader of the Labour Party, even though Wilson had pinpricked him, which hurt at the time. There was also a personal message given to Mrs Sherriff.

Though Gaitskell has, it seems, made only rare spirit returns, he also manifested on one occasion to journalist Anne Dooley. Miss Dooley knew the Labour leader professionally when she was a Fleet Street industrial correspondent. At that time she frequently met him when he was Minister of Fuel and Power.

Gaitskell communicated halfway through a sitting Miss Dooley had with medium Stewart Lawson. He correctly predicted a Labour victory in the 1964 election, warning, 'It will not be easy.'

Some years earlier, it transpired that another Socialist leader, Clement Attlee, had a strange psychic gift. When a Labour MP's wife told him of her spirit healing faculty, Attlee confessed 'to some direct talent in the same direction.' He was, he claimed, a wart healer, and his family were usually treated by him with success. Whether he cured political warts was not mentioned!

It is also relevant to include Attlee's comments regarding legislation to put Spiritualism on a legal footing and allow mediums to practise openly.

'The Labour Party,' he said, 'stands for the complete freedom and equality of all religious bodies. I should, therefore, be in favour of freeing Spiritualists from restrictions on their liberty and of repealing obsolete Acts. I . . . would support legislation designed to give freedom under proper conditions to those engaged in psychic research.'

Turning to political leaders of a different complexion, eligible and long-time batchelor Edward Heath unwittingly and probably unknowingly proved one wrong. During a Commonwealth Conference in Singapore, a local fortune-teller, Tommy Eng, using centuries-old sand from China, an egg timer and some curious incantations, predicted that Heath would announce his engagement the following July. Mr Eng did, however, score more accurately with former Canadian Premier Pierre Trudeau. He foretold his engagement—and got the month correct.

Lastly, no chapter on Premiers' psychic stories would be complete without including Margaret Thatcher.

According to one report, seer Simon Alexander offered the 'Iron Maiden' some advice on Britain's ailing economy. It was reported that Alexander, then thirty-eight, was invited by one of the Premier's top aides to send his recovery masterplan to No 10. The request, said the claim, came from Derek Howe, of the Government Political Office. 'I will make sure Mrs Thatcher sees it without delay,' was his reported response.

Four years earlier Alexander appeared at a bankruptcy court. He admitted liabilities of over £17,000 when his assets were £55 and a crystal ball. Eamon Murphy, the assistant official receiver, told the seer: 'You were going down the slippery slope. You did not need to be clairvoyant to see where you were going.' Alexander countered: 'If I look into the future, I see only what I want to see. Human nature takes over. No one wants to see the problems facing him. But I am now fated to become rich and famous in five years' time.'

Other authorities have delved deeper in Mrs Thatcher's life . . . or rather her past lives. According to Dr Douglas Baker, the director of a Potters Bar, Herts., college devoted to matters psychic and esoteric,

Mrs Thatcher was a reincarnation of the Black Prince. Dr Baker's assertion was based on astrology and meditation. 'There's even a great similarity in the shapes of their faces,' he said. 'They both have very high cheekbones.'

What's more, two trade union chiefs were asked to comment. 'I reckon she was Anne Boleyn,' said one, 'all charm and no head,' while another stated, 'She reminds me of Salome, because of her obsession with capital cuts.' A Labour MP added, 'When you look at the cuts she is making in the health service, she's the cruellest woman since Lady Macbeth.' Others have claimed that Mrs Thatcher was once a nun. Apparently, her astrological chart 'really is ultra-sensitive, still retaining her nun-like qualities.'

Fascinatingly, before she became PM, two other journals cast Mrs Thatcher's chart. One reported it contained 'all the indications of considerable additional responsibility, power and change. These seem to point to her achieving the highest office on which she sets her sights.'

The other ominously warned that Mrs Thatcher could expect 'serious troubles with colleagues, the sort of thing that brings intrigue and scandal . . . if she became Prime Minister her type of virtue would show itself in the life of the country.'

Finally, the Prime Minister's much-reported eye illness proved Bexleyheath, Kent, clairvoyant Nella Jones right. Before the last election, Nella told a reporter that not only would Mrs Thatcher win it, but that the Premier would be out of action soon afterwards because of a health problem.

In addition, Nella forecast on one of her regular early-morning TV spots that Mrs Thatcher's condition would occur six weeks to two months after the country cast its votes. 'I was spot on,' said Nella afterwards. When a reporter phoned her after the TV prediction was made, 'I told him the trouble would be in some way connected with a head illness.' Though her eyesight was not permanently impaired, Mrs Thatcher underwent medical treatment to correct a problem. And for Nella, at least, it was another bull's-eye so to speak.

QUEEN ELIZABETH, THE QUEEN MOTHER: She gave a well-known medium a gold brooch as a thank you gift after attending sittings.

TOM CORBETT: *A national Sunday newspaper published a retraction that he was consulted by the Queen Mother.*

QUEEN VICTORIA: Though nicknamed "The Widow of Windsor," many claim that she, too, attended seances.

JOHN BROWN: Many maintain that he was Queen Victoria's trusted medium. The monarch once called him "God's own gift."

HARRY EDWARDS: Various members of the Royal family, notably Princess Marie Louise, consulted him for spirit healing.

WINSTON CHURCHILL: He told of psychic experiences more than once.

F. D. ROOSEVELT: According to one famous medium he attended his own funeral service.

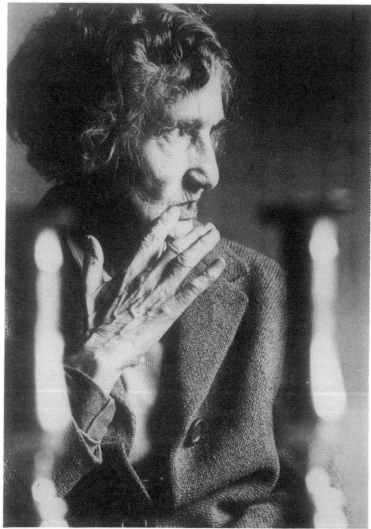

GERALDINE CUMMINS: Using her automatic writing gift, she gave Canadian Premier Mackenzie King spirit messages from his mother and President Roosevelt.

JOSEF STALIN: He ordered a psychic to "rob" a major Moscow bank and obtain 100,000 roubles.

NICHOLAS II: He wrote that Rasputin, the so-called mad monk, "made a remarkably strong impression both on Her Majesty and myself."

Spiritual Statesmen

AS INTERNATIONAL SPIRITUAL statesmen, Popes are held in esteem throughout the world not only by devout Roman Catholics, but politicians and leaders of many nations no matter what their political complexion. Despite their seeming antagonism towards psychic matters, Pontiffs are on record as having experienced visions, and even, some say, participating in seances.

According to press accounts not only in Britain but also abroad, there is evidence that Pope Paul VI, who died in 1978 after a massive heart attack, was no stranger to psychic phenomena. Indeed, he was said to accept without reservation the authenticity of tape-recorded spirit communications that were played to him and other prelates in the Vatican.

But was he aware of the fact that in 1975 a Papal Nuncio had a three-hour sitting with British psychic healer Matthew Manning when a diagnosis of his health—close colleagues were concerned about—was given in automatic writing? It came from Thomas Penn, the pseudonym used by a 19th-century physician whose identity the Vatican was instrumental in helping to establish. Penn wrote via Manning.

Publisher Peter Bander, who has a very close relationship with the Roman Catholic Church—he has written a book on the Pontiffs—said in *Psychic News* that Pope Paul VI was 'spiritually very highly aware.'

The first hint of the Pope's serious illness came when he cancelled his usual audience on Sunday. He had never done this before, though he had suffered from failing health for some years.

The *Daily Mirror* said that some Vatican observers felt the Pope, already frail and weak, was badly affected by the shock he suffered over the kidnapping and killing of his friend, former Italian Premier Aldo

Moro. Later the Pontiff told a friend in the Vatican, 'We hope to meet him after death, which for us cannot be far away.'

The first news about Matthew Manning's automatic writing diagnosis appeared in the *News of the World*. Its story stated that mystery surrounded 'the visit of two top Vatican emissaries to Britain's leading psychic, Matthew Manning.' The paper added that the Roman Catholic Apostolic Delegation in Britain said the visit soon after Matthew's appearance on David Frost's TV show was purely social.

'But,' the report continued, 'Matthew's friends are convinced the real purpose was to see, in a roundabout way, if the psychic could throw any light on the state of the Pope's health.' Matthew told the reporter: 'They asked me to make certain diagnoses using birth dates. I need only a person's birth date for this kind of work. They handed me a list of about fifty dates. I later learned one was that of the present Pope.'

The emissaries were named as Archbishop Hyginus Cardinale, a top Vatican diplomat, and the present Apostolic Delegate to Britain, Monsignor Bruno Heim.

After the Frost show Matthew was invited with Bander to Monsignor Heim's Wimbledon, SW London, home. On 2nd November Archbishop Cardinale flew into Britain with Monsignor Heim and saw Matthew at Bander's Gerrards Cross, Bucks, home.

It was then the fifty birth dates were produced. One date stuck in Bander's mind. He recognised it as Pontiff's.

'Both Bander and Matthew,' said the reporter, 'are reluctant to discuss details of the diagnosis of this date, but I understand it was serious.' Monsignor Heim was quoted as saying: 'It is true that Archbishop Cardinale and I met Matthew Manning. But we didn't consult him about the Pope's health. If you say so, it would seriously embarrass me. I would have to deny it.'

A few weeks later *Psychic News* printed an account headlined, 'Inside story of top Vatican emissaries' seances revealed.' It was based on disclosures made in an interview in a Swedish periodical, *Hemmets Journal*. Interviewed was Friedrich Jurgenson, a Roman Catholic who is regarded as the 'discoverer' of the electronic voice phenomenon. The theory behind this is that spirit voices can be tape recorded.

A film producer, writer, artist and medium, Jurgenson first heard the supernormal voices in his Swedish flat in 1956. Since then he has demonstrated that his tape-recordings include spirit messages from identified communicators.

His interview revealed that a wind of change was blowing through the Vatican, which for years was officially hostile to seance phenomena. Closely associated with the Vatican, in 1969 Pope Paul VI decorated Jurgenson with the Commander's Cross of the Order of St Gregory the Great. Jurgenson was previously interviewed by Peter Bander in the now defunct *Psychic Researcher*, which he then edited.

Bander asked how did the Vatican, the Pope, cardinals and archbishops react to Jurgenson's declaration that he had received 'voices from the dead.' The reply was that the then Pope and two others before him had listened sympathetically on many occasions to his recital of this phenomenon. 'I have demonstrated it time and time again,' said Jurgenson. 'They accepted it without reservation.' He had played some of his tape-recordings to the Pope and other prelates.

In *Hemmets Journal* the reporter told Jurgenson that what seemed to be of special interest to the two prelates mentioned in the *News of the World* account was the serious state of the Pope's health; there had been rumours for the previous two years about his health and even speculation that he might abdicate.

Naturally, added the writer, the *News of the World* account was of interest to millions of Roman Catholics. The story would probably have fizzled out had it not been for its being denied in the *Catholic Herald*. There Archbishop Heim said it was absolutely unthinkable that the Vatican should consult Matthew. But, said the journalist, it seemed the newspaper was correct in asserting that the Vatican had consulted Matthew and the spirit doctor.

That year Jurgenson had spent a week in London. He stayed at the Apostolic Delegation, the Vatican's Embassy in Britain, with Archbishop Heim. Jurgenson said that he was present when Matthew was invited to the archbishop's home. He was also with the archbishop when he went to Bander's home to meet Matthew.

It would not be honest to keep quiet about the facts. He saw no reason to be timorous; psychic experiments were made on those occasions. The Roman Catholic Church was quite open to these phenomena. Why should it not be interested in afterlife evidence?

Jurgenson was asked the kind of experiments done in the Papal Nuncio's presence. He said that what happened was fantastic. They established a direct connection between a message Matthew received in automatic writing and a voice that came on Jurgenson's tape recorder. It was the first time this had happened. Archbishop Heim was very impressed.

Did Matthew make any Thomas Penn diagnosis? he was asked. Not at that time, was the reply. On the Papal Nuncio's request, he had done so previously. Among others there was one for the Pope from his birth date. Jurgenson did not know the result. To him there was nothing sensational about this. The Church was in close contact with psychical research. Every year it arranged a conference on this subject in Germany. Among participants there was a Roman Catholic priest who received messages from former Popes by the electronic voice phenomenon.

Finally, said the journalist, there was an ironic twist. Archbishop Heim's denial was given prominence in a *Catholic Herald* front page. Yet by coincidence in another column it reported what the Pope said about psychics to an open-air audience of 50,000. He told them all that Christians were not called on to dedicate themselves to experiencing these extraordinary phenomena which characterised exceptional men and women, some of whom the Church had honoured.

Turning to other Pontiffs, one Italian sculptor claimed he was visited by the apparition of Leo XIII. The phantom blessed him and then melted away. The sculptor told the then Pope, who is said to have replied: 'Be grateful, my son, that my illustrious predecessor visited thee. He often comes to me. When I am in doubt concerning how to proceed in some case, I write a question, leaving it upon the writing desk in my study, and the next morning I find the answer written below my question in the handwriting of his deceased Holiness.'

Some years later an American medium Loe F. Elmore, asserted that Pope Pius IX talked with the 'dead' of his own family, his sister acting as the medium. In her memoirs, Mrs Elmore recorded: 'I made the friendship of a very dear English lady, Cecilia Cockburn-Campbell, a Roman Catholic, while I was in Melbourne. She was an earnest student of Spiritualism. On learning that I expected to visit some of the art centres of Italy, when I left Melbourne, she gave me a letter of introduction to the President of the Irish College in Rome. He was to arrange for me to have an audience with Pope Pius IX.

'It was common knowledge, among the Catholics, that His Excellency believed in the communication between the living and the so-called dead. Upon reaching Rome, I presented my letter of

introduction. Father O'Reardon welcomed me warmly. We talked of
Spiritualism, for my letter introduced me as a Spiritualist teacher.

'When I was about to leave, he said: "You will receive the day after
tomorrow an invitation to the Vatican, from the Secretary of the Pope.
You will be interviewed by him first, then he will tell you what day and
hour you will be received by His Excellency.

'The invitation was delivered to my hotel. I was invited to visit the
Secretary of the Pope the next day. I assure you that I arrived on time. I
was received most cordially. We talked of Spiritualism, and when he
learned that I could not speak Italian, he said: "That is too bad, for His
Excellency speaks only a little French, besides his own language. I am
sure he would be happy to talk with you for he is keenly interested in
psychic phenomena.

' "One of his sisters is a medium, and they often hold communion
with their loved ones who have passed on." The next day I received an
invitation to be at the Pope's Palace at the hour of noon. I was received
by a cardinal, and escorted to the reception hall. The beauty, the
richness, I can never forget. The recognition of my knowledge of spirit
return was in the eyes of His Holiness after the audience was over.'

In fairness it must be added that this story was fiercely refuted by the
Universe Roman Catholic journal. It dismissed the account as 'too
ridiculous for refutation,' adding: 'It was under Pope Pius IX and with
his approval that the Holy Office in 1856 condemned the evocation of
departed spirits "and other superstitious practices" and exhorted the
Bishops to put forth every effort to suppress these abuses. There have
been other prohibitions since then.'

Be that as it may, it was reported that in 1950 during four
consecutive walks in the Vatican gardens, Pope Pius XII experienced
a series of visions. They were described by a cardinal as 'apparitions'
of the Virgin Mary. Similarly in 1955, during a severe illness, it
was officially stated that the Pontiff saw 'the sweet personality of
Jesus Christ' at his bedside. The Pope, who was expecting to die,
heard the words, 'true and distinct,' of the voice of Jesus announcing
that his hour of death had not yet come. This experience was
described by the Vatican as a 'supernatural event.' Earlier, the Pope was
credited with healing powers in that he restored the sight of a blind boy
and girl.

More extravagant claims were made by leading Spiritualist Arthur
Findlay. Several high church dignitaries were said to be present when

in 1934 he gave an address on Spiritualism to a large audience in Rome. Findlay maintained that a cardinal, with whom he talked after the meeting, told him that seances were held at the Vatican. The cardinal added that Pope Pius XI was such a bad seance-room sitter that much better results were obtained when he was not present.

Mention must also be made of Pope John XXIII who died after a reign of less than five years. As his illness took its final course the Pontiff said: 'I have been able to follow my death step by step. Now I am going gently toward the end.' Outside the Vatican devout Roman Catholics knelt in prayer. Their clothes were drenched with rain, their faces tear-stained. Inside Pope John was telling those around his death-bed that he accepted God's will. Then, with simplicity, he added, 'With death begins a new life.' Soon he was to experience it first hand . . .

Turning to today, few would argue that Pope John Paul II is the world's most popular and prayed for Pontiff. Of course, there is a certain wry irony that communist-dominated Poland is his birthplace. What is even more ironic is that a British spirit healer has healed and been seen by hundreds of thousands of Poles during the last few years. The healer's name, unknown to most even in Britain, is Clive Harris. One can only wonder whether the present Pope knows of his activities. Surely he must for Harris's following within his native land is unparalleled. During one of the shy, soft-spoken healer's visits in 1979 he ministered to a staggering 25,000 people daily, according to a *New York Times* reporter. Among his eager patients were not only ordinary, every-day folk, but nuns, priests, medical students and, it was rumoured, high Communist Party officials. It was estimated that during his three-week visit 450,000 patients would seek Harris's aid.

So startling were the results of his behind the Iron Curtain visit that three hundred volunteers sifted applications for six weeks. Free tickets were marked with Government identification numbers to prevent a black market trade in the passes. In 1978 illicitly-gained tickets sold for £15. Thousands waited hours in the bitter cold to seek Clive's help; farmers drove hundreds of miles for treatment; terminal patients from hospital were taken by ambulance to him for healing.

In his 'special' report, the journalist, writing from Warsaw, said the 'faith healing' phenomenon was 'sweeping' Poland in the shape of the 'thin, intense, curly-haired miracle-worker' Harris.

Three months earlier a small sign had appeared on the interior courtyard of Warsaw's St Jacques Dominican Church and Monastery. Sufferers were invited to submit applications to see Clive. 'It was the only printed notice that he would visit,' said the paper. The Church was besieged by a tumultuous crowd, estimated by Harris's assistants, and confirmed by the number of printed tickets issued, at 25,000 a day. Long queues 'snaked along the cobbled streets of the Gothic-styled New Town. Thousands waited patiently in the bitter cold as long as five hours for that appointed moment in which they would file past Harris and feel the touch of his long, slender fingers.'

This kind of healing was new to Poland, the report said. Judging from its attraction 'it has struck a responsive chord among the deeply religious, predominantly Roman Catholic population. At the same time it would appear to be an anachronism for a Government that follows the path of scientific socialism and adheres to Marxist principles of rationality in human affairs.' Harris, who accepts no money or gifts, was now 'famous' in Poland, 'universally referred to by his given name.'

The 1979 visit was organised by brothers Maximilian and Benedict Bylicki. They predicted Clive would see 450,000 in his three-week stay, which would include Poland's major cities.

'When we began four years ago we had 100 people,' said Maximilian, a musician, who clicked a counter incessantly as the crowd surged around him. 'We had 500 and then 1,000. We were afraid. How were we going to handle all these people? Now we get 30,000 a day. We are not afraid at all.' Maximilian presided over 300 volunteers, many of them Roman Catholic youth group members. To control the crowds, the volunteers used walkie-talkies, barricades and other paraphernalia.

Neither of Poland's two major institutions, the Roman Catholic Church and Communist Party, gave public notice to Clive. 'But,' said the reporter, 'his ability to get visas to come from his London home twice a year and to hold his audiences in a church refectory are taken as sure signs that the Central Committee and the episcopate lend tacit approval to his activities.'

In 1978 the weekly Marxist *Polityka* carried a long article that tried to weigh the results and determine whether Clive cured the sick or not. People advanced diverse theories to substantiate Clive's gift. Some maintained his hands emit radioactive rays; others thought 'biomagnetism' was responsible.

Others believed the primary effect was psychological, but the results were still valid, 'especially for cases so severe that they are given up as lost by physicians.'

'What is striking,' said the *New York Times*, 'is that the patients are from all walks of life. The head of a pediatric unit at a major Warsaw hospital is said to have consulted Harris. Rumours circulate that high party officials have appeared.' One assistant said that at night 'limousines pull up.'

Clive worked from 6.00 a.m. to midnight without a break. The line of sufferers moved past him constantly. Each patient held a card listing in English the ailment's site. Clive touched sufferers for less than a second. He grimaced in concentration before moving on to the next person.

In 1981 *The Observer* brought Harris to its liberal-minded readers' attention. Then Harris's tour took him to Gdansk, Slypsk, Szczecin and towns in the rural south. 'Rumours abound,' said a journalist reporting the tour, 'the most potent being that he once cured President Brezhnev.'

Harris's healing sessions, the paper added, 'are an impressive sight.' Around 9,000 people packed into Warsaw's St Jacek's Church for one meeting. Patients stood in long queues, often for as long as five hours. They held cards describing in English what ailed them. Clive merely passed his hand over the affected area without saying a word. In case any were overcome by the experience a medical team stood by.

One supporter said Clive did not work miracles. Some reported complete, spontaneous cures. Cited was the case of a woman who had sores on her legs that doctors were unable to heal. She saw Harris—and they went. A year later the healer was swamped by an astonishing 300,000 people. In something of a scoop, the German psychic magazine *Esotera* printed three pictures of one of Clive's visits. They were taken by Polish photographer Andrej Polec, who accompanied Clive. Clive then visited eighteen of the country's largest cities. These included Warsaw, Katowice, Szczecin, Gdansk, Wroclaw and Lodz.

Esotera said that wherever he visited, long queues formed. An average of 10,000 to 15,000 people daily went to see the healer.

The authorities did not try to hinder Clive in any way. Most of his healing demonstrations were given in churches. The Roman Catholic Church organised and publicised the tour in co-operation with members of the Polish aristocracy. The Church bore all the costs. 'Clive Harris did not accept any fees for treating the sick who sought his help in Poland,' said the journal. Many people reported improvement after spirit healing. The healer stayed only one day in each city and was given hospitality in the homes of Roman Catholic clerics.

Andrej Polec said that those who thronged the healer reacted in a 'very religious way.' There were even shouts of 'Jesus has come to Poland.'

Antoni Starza, a Pole now living in Britain, explained to me why Clive is so popular in Poland and why he is supported by the Roman Catholic Church and aristocracy.

'Poland, although predominantly Roman Catholic, was never averse to psychic and spiritual phenomena,' said Mr Starza. 'After all Ossowiecki, possibly one of the greatest psychics of all time, was Polish and active in Poland. Even before the First World War psychic investigations were carried out in places like Warsaw and Lwow.'

Mr Starza thought one reason why Poles are so favourable in their attitude towards healers lies in the history of the country. 'Poland is largely agricultural,' he said. 'There was the good wise woman in each village. You could not describe her as a Spiritualist, but she knew something about healing.'

People in every village, he added, also knew about faculties such as dowsing. Since healing 'was not practised as a religion the Church never pronounced against it.'

Mr Starza explained healing, rightly regarded as a natural phenomenon, was almost taken for granted in Poland. Asked if Clive was so popular because of any failure of the medical profession in Poland Mr Starza said: 'Under the Communists everything is in a bad state. Doctors are trying to get as much help as they can. Any kind of healing would be to some extent a substitution or addition to medicine.'

Mr Starza added: 'Doctors have never been hostile to healing. For example, they know all about herbal medicine and sometimes prefer it to tablets or pills. The Communist authorities are more against psychic phenomena than the Church, at least publicly.'

Because of the Solidarity struggle Poland, has, of course, been much in the news in recent years. To outsiders it still appears to be a torn, turbulent, nation. Yet even during the period when martial law was in force Clive Harris still toured Poland ministering to the sick.

Frankly, if you saw the healer walking down his local High Road you would not look twice. Nothing outwardly distinguishes him from his less psychically-endowed mortals. When in Britain Harris lives in Wembley, Middlesex. Always he refuses press interviews and questions from prying journalists; always he refuses to discuss his Polish visits; always he remains quietly in the background. Perhaps he, too, like Pope John Paul II has found in Poland his spiritual home and a measure of inner serenity.

Seen in Vision

THERE ARE TIMES in history when the world, because of some shattering, devastating event, momentarily stops. A sort of pallor covers nations. One subject is on everyone's lips. Usually it is a tragedy, one of monumental proportions. One that will effect the days to come. One that will forever be recorded in history books. One that casts a sickening shadow over humanity.

Such an event was the assassination of John F. Kennedy. The world plunged into mourning. An indication of the effect Kennedy's passing had is that if you ask anyone over the age of thirty-five and over what they were doing when they heard of the President's death they can usually remember. Straightaway. Without any thought. The event is indelibly marked upon their lives. Yet Kennedy's killing in Dallas in 1963 was foreseen by a famous American psychic some years before.

The seer in question is Jeane Dixon. She is also credited with predicting the date of Roosevelt's death at his own request in a secret White House session. It was in 1956 that a magazine reporter asked Mrs Dixon to forecast the result of the 1960 Presidential election. Her chillingly accurate reply was: 'It will be dominated by labour and won by a Democrat. But he will be assassinated or die in office, though not necessarily in his first term.'

Later it transpired that Mrs Dixon experienced a vivid vision concerning Kennedy in 1952 while she was praying in St Matthew's Cathedral. She 'saw' a young, tall, blue-eyed Democratic President. Next a voice said he would be elected to power in 1960, but die while in office.

After Kennedy's election, Mrs Dixon began 'seeing' the assassination . . . before it occurred. She told people as the day drew near, asking that a warning be conveyed to him. When he was shot, Alice Roosevelt Longworth, President Roosevelt's daughter, is said to have telephoned

Washington hostess Kay Halle and told her: 'Turn on your radio quickly. It has happened, as Jean Dixon said it would.'

There is also ample evidence that Mrs Dixon's preview was well-known in top circles. Three days before Kennedy's assassination, Mrs Dixon stated categorically, 'The President is going to be shot.' Journalist John Gold spoke to half a dozen reputable men and women who testified that in the preceding weeks Mrs Dixon had repeatedly referred to a White House tragedy. Three witnesses stated she had specifically forecast Kennedy's imminent death. One, a former US naval officer and retired White House bandmaster, said that on the Tuesday before the killing she suddenly startled friends with whom she was dining by saying, 'The President is going to be shot.' Before that Mrs Dixon repeatedly spoke of seeing 'a dark cloud' hovering over the White House. Later she added, 'The veil is drawing together.'

Mrs Dixon—at that time she had correctly predicted every Presidential election in the past two decades—told John Gold that the previous weekend when she drove past the White House, 'I had a vision of the building draped in black. It got worse over the next few days. On Tuesday, while having dinner, I "saw" the President shot before my eyes . . . On the day of his death I was having breakfast with an old friend. By this time the White House was completely veiled in black.' I said, "Charles, this is the day, this is the day when it has to happen." It did.'

Best-selling novelist Taylor Caldwell also claims to have forecast Kennedy's death. 'I have had many prophetic dreams which always come true,' she said. In June 1963 Miss Caldwell dreamed she was watching TV in the lounge. She 'saw' Kennedy murdered and watched him falling to his left. Her vision came in colour. The President was wearing a medium grey suit, striped tie and was hatless.

On waking, Miss Caldwell ran downstairs to the dining room. The cook was serving her husband's breakfast. 'The President has been murdered . . .' the writer exclaimed. Miss Caldwell went into the lounge, turned on the TV set and was puzzled because the usual programmes were being transmitted. In great despair, recognising the dream as a warning, Miss Caldwell wrote to the White House. She and Kennedy had already corresponded. 'He wrote me gracious and soothing letters in reply,' she said.

As the President would not take her warning seriously, Miss Caldwell submitted an article for *The Wanderer*, published in St Paul,

Minnesota. She referred to the probable assassination as happening very shortly. It was published in October 1963 'with a gentle and indulgent raising of eyebrows.' The article was headed, 'President Kennedy in danger?' Other newspapers followed up the story and where equally amused. Yet the following month Kennedy was killed exactly as Miss Caldwell previewed five months earlier.

During the intervening period, the writer, like Mrs Dixon, told many friends about her dream. Because so many newspapers featured her prophecy Miss Caldwell was visited by the Secret Service. 'How did I know?' she asked. 'I do not know. It is one of the thousands of other similar predictions.'

Lastly there is also evidence that celebrated American medium Arthur Ford previewed the tragic events at Dallas. Journalist Ruth Montgomery joined eight Protestant clergymen and a doctor at a Ford seance held in Washington. During the seance, Fletcher, the medium's spirit guide, reminded those present that a year beforehand he had told Miss Montgomery the President would die.

The journalist recalled she had tape-recorded that sitting. She played it back and heard the guide, who entranced Ford, state that Kennedy would die by 'falling in a moving vehicle.' Miss Montgomery later explained she had forgotten the incident because she interpreted it to mean an aeroplane crash.

Though it is probably coincidence the President himself uttered some strangely and sadly prophetic words a mere three hours before he died. A seven-man commission into his death heard that he stated: 'If anybody really wants to shoot the President of the United States it is not a very difficult job. All one has to do is to get a high building some day with a telescopic rifle and there is nothing anybody can do to defend against such an attempt.'

Of Roosevelt many claims have been made concerning his psychic interest. Indeed, the Rev O. R. Washburn wrote: 'It is known among friends of mine, and known beyond question, that the former President of the United States, several members of his Cabinet and the heads of important departments at Washington secured very good mediums, held many seances, listened carefully to suggestions made by former Presidents, generals, admirals and diplomats now residing in the spirit world.'

The cleric continued: 'When President Roosevelt was Governor of New York he was much interested in a plan for a well-known institution, with professors and the usual equipment, founded to study advanced psychology and employing mediums at stated salaries. His entry into national campaigns caused him to abandon his interest in this matter.'

Following the President's death at least two writers used language with a psychic flavour concerning Roosevelt. R. J. Cruikshank said that like Lincoln 'he seemed to possess a mediumistic quality about men, policies and events.' Secondly, Sir Philip Gibbs told of a visit to the White House during the black days of the Second World War. He found Roosevelt 'serene, cheerful and utterly confident of final victory. It was not a pose, as I could see. He was like a clairvoyant who saw the future in a clear and shining vision.' Of the President's personality, he added, 'There was something strange about it, something almost supernatural.'

On an amusing note, a few years earlier Joseph Davis, then American Ambassador at Brussels, addressed the Eisteddfod. He brought a Presidential message in which he was meant to say, 'Your Welshmen are famous for their spirituality.' Instead he said '. . . are famous for their Spiritualism.' Back to more down-to-earth matters, famous British journalist Hannen Swaffer claimed at a public meeting held in Brighton, Sussex, that during the war a medium was flown regularly from the West Coast of America to Washington to give sittings to Roosevelt.

Earlier, in a newspaper dated 17th February 1932, it was stated that Mrs Roosevelt 'for the first time in her life . . . consulted a Spiritualist. Governor Roosevelt, preferring to hear the revelation secondhand, remained outside the room.' As a 'last minute inspiration,' Mrs Roosevelt invited medium Margaret Lewis to give readings at an exclusive party.

The report added: 'While professional ethics prevent Mrs Lewis from discussing more questions asked her by Mrs Roosevelt, she was willing to explain the reason for the cheerful smile the Governor's wife wore when she rejoined her guests. Mrs Roosevelt's first question was whether her husband will receive the nomination for President and, if so, whether he will be elected. The reply was that there will be other strong contenders for the nomination, but that Governor Roosevelt will probably get it.' He did.

When pressed for more details, Mrs Lewis said that Mrs Roosevelt not only asked her to demonstrate clairvoyance, but sent a 6ft 2in state trooper, two police cars and a limousine so she would be properly escorted to her destination. At that time this was the only case on record where a medium was invited to the Governor's Albany mansion. Furthermore, a local paper printed a picture of the medium standing beside 'Mrs F.D.R.'

But what of Roosevelt's spirit returns? It is known that Canadian Premier Mackenzie King certainly accepted seance communications from him. He received messages from Roosevelt through British automatic writing medium Geraldine Cummins. Of one message describing how the President had met Mackenzie King's mother in the spirit world, the Premier commented, 'The phrases he used, the characterisation, were exactly what I'd have expected from Franklyn Roosevelt if he'd met my mother in life.'

According to Miss Cummins's seance writings from Roosevelt only his dog paid any attention at his funeral! The communicator said to be the President wrote: 'Wish I could give one more fireside talk to tell the American people the greatest humbug of all is death . . . I was very active at my funeral. The only one who paid any attention to me at that funeral was Scottie, my dog. I was very amused at all the best brains in the country concentrating on that shabby old garment of mine that was being put under the earth and there I, large as life, and when my dog saw me he rolled on the ground, making quite a diversion. I went into a body like my own body, young, healthy, strong, and no one at my funeral saw me because this body was travelling a little faster than theirs.'

Obviously, in the long roll call of American Presidents and statesmen some names stand out supreme. Take George Washington and Benjamin Franklin. Even today, many years after their deaths, their names instil a certain pride. But how many know that Washington, for example, recorded the details of a vision which, transcending time, space and ordinary human understanding, showed him 'the birth, progress and destiny of the United States?'

That this vivid psychic experience had a profound effect on Washington, 'The son of the Republic,' cannot be refuted. Here is how he described the happening, during which he saw and heard details and words normally beyond the reach of our five very limited physical senses:

'I do not know whether it is owing to the anxiety of my mind, or what but this afternoon, as I was sitting at this table . . . engaged in preparing a dispatch, something seemed to disturb me. Looking up, I beheld standing opposite me . . . a singularly beautiful female. So astonished was I, for I had given strict orders . . . not to be disturbed, that it was some moments before I found language to inquire the cause of her presence.

'A second, a third, and even a fourth time, did I repeat my question, but received no answer from my 'mysterious' visitor, except a slight raising of her eyes. By this time, I felt strange sensations spreading through me. I would have risen, but the riveted gaze of the being before me rendered volition impossible.

'I assayed once more to address her, but my tongue had become useless. Even thought itself had become paralysed. A new influence, mysterious, potent, irresistible, took possession of me. All I could do was to gaze steadily, vacantly, at my unknown visitant.

'Gradually the surrounding atmosphere, seemed as though becoming filled with sensations, and grew luminous. Everything about me seemed to rarify, the mysterious visitor herself becoming more airy and yet more distinct to my sight than before.

'I now began to feel as one dying, or rather to experience the sensation which I have sometimes imagined accompanies dissolution. I did not think, I did not reason, I did not move; all were alike impossible. I was only conscious of gazing fixedly, vacantly, at my companion. Presently I heard an etheric voice . . . saying, "Son of the republic, look and learn," while at the same time, my visitor extended her arm eastwardly. I now beheld a heavy white vapour at some distance, rising . . . fold upon fold.

'This gradually dissipated and I looked upon a strange scene. Before me lay spread out in one vast plain all the countries of the world . . . Europe, Asia, Africa and America. I saw rolling and tossing between Europe and America the billows of the Atlantic, and between Asia and America . . . lay the Pacific.

'"Son of the republic," said the same spirit-like voice as before, "look and learn." At that moment I beheld a dark, shadowy being, like an angel, standing, or rather floating, in mid-air, between Europe and America. Dipping water out of the ocean in the hollow of each hand, he sprinkled some upon America with his right hand, while with his left he cast some on Europe.

'Immediately, a cloud raised from these countries and joined in mid-ocean. For a while, it remained stationary, and then moved slowly westward . . . until it enveloped America in its murky folds. Sharp flashes of lightning gleamed through it at intervals, and I heard the smothered groans and cries of the American people.

'A second time the angel dipped water from the ocean and sprinkled it out as before. The dark cloud was then drawn back to the ocean, in whose heaving billows it sank from view. A third time I heard the same identical voice saying, "Son of the republic, look and learn."

'I cast my eyes upon America and beheld villages and towns and cities, springing up one after another, until the whole land from the Atlantic to the Pacific was dotted with them. Again I heard the mysterious voice say: "Son of the republic, the end of the century cometh. Look and learn." And then the dark, shadowy angel turned his face southward, and, from Africa, I saw an ill-omened spectre approach our land. It flitted slowly over every town and city of the latter. The inhabitants presently set themselves in battle array against each other.

'As I continued looking, I saw a bright angel, on whose brow rested a crown of light, on which was traced the word "Union," bearing the American flag, which he placed between the divided nation and said, "Remember ye are brethren." Instantly the inhabitants, casting from them . . . their weapons, became friends once more and united around the national standard.

'And again I heard the voice saying, "Son of the republic, look and learn." At this the dark, shadowy angel placed a trumpet to his mouth and blew three distinct blasts, and taking water from the ocean, he sprinkled it upon Europe, Asia and Africa.

'Then my eyes beheld a fearful scene, from each of these countries arose thick, black clouds that were soon joined into one. And throughout this mass . . . there gleamed a dark red light by which I saw hordes of armed men, who, moving with the cloud, marched by land and sailed by sea to America, which country was enveloped in the volume of cloud. And I dimly saw these vast armies devastate the whole country and burn the villages, towns and cities that I beheld springing up. As my ears listened to the thundering of the cannon, clashing of swords and the shouts and cries of millions in mortal combat, I again heard the spirit voice saying, "Son of the republic, look and learn." When the voice had ceased, the dark, shadowy angel placed his trumpet once more to his mouth and blew a long and fearful blast. Instantly a light, as of a thousand suns, shone down from above me and pierced and broke into fragments the dark cloud which enveloped America. At the same moment the angel upon whose head still shone the words "Union," and who bore our national flag in one hand and a sword in the other, descended from the heavens attended by legions of white spirits. These immediately joined the inhabitants of America, who, I perceived, were well nigh overcome, but who immediately, taking courage again, closed up their broken ranks and renewed the battle. Again, amid the fearful noise of the conflict, I heard the same spirit voice saying, "Son of the republic, look and learn." As the voice ceased, the shadowy angel for the last time dipped water from the ocean and sprinkled it upon America. Instantly, the dark cloud rolled back, together with the armies it had brought, leaving the inhabitants of the land victorious.

'Then once more I beheld the villages, towns and cities, springing up where I had seen them before, while the bright angel, planting the azure standard he had brought in the midst of them, cried with a loud voice, "While the stars remain, and the heavens send down dew upon the earth . . . so long shall the union last." And taking, from his brow, the crown on which blazoned the word "Union," he placed it upon the standard . . . while the people, kneeling down, said "Amen."

'The scene instantly began to fade and dissolve, and I at last saw nothing but the rising, curling vapour . . . I at first beheld. This also disappearing, I found myself once more . . . gaping upon the mysterious visitor who, in the same voice I had heard before . . . said: "Son of the republic, what you have seen is thus interpreted. Three great perils will come upon the republic. The most fearful is the third passing which the whole world united shall not prevail against. Let every child of the republic learn to live for his God, his land and union." With these words . . . the vision vanished, and I started from my seat and felt that I had seen a vision wherein had been shown me the birth, progress and destiny of the United States.'

Benjamin Franklin, still one of America's most famous citizens, also believed in mankind's spiritual nature as is apparent from a letter he wrote to a relative following his brother's death. Doubtless trying to assuage the relative's grief he wrote assuringly: 'A man is not completely born until he is dead. Why then should we grieve that a new child is born among the immortals?

'We are spirits. That bodies should be lent us, while they can afford us pleasure, assist us in acquiring knowledge or in doing good to our fellow creatures, is a kind and benevolent act of God. When they become unfit for these purposes and afford us pain instead of pleasure, instead of an aid become an encumbrance, it is equally kind and benevolent that a way is provided by which we may get rid of them. Death is that way. 'Our friend and we were invited abroad on a party of pleasure which is to last for ever. His chair was ready first and he is gone before us. We could not all conveniently start together; and why should you and I be grieved at this, since we are soon to follow and know where to find him?' Franklin, born in 1706, died in 1790. For ten years a member of the General Assembly, he lived in Britain for eighteen years. On returning to America, he helped to frame the Constitution.

Of the White House, America's most famous building, stories abound of spectres being sighted, spectres of past presidents. Harry Truman told writer Leslie Lieber that at times of national calamity, some staff members insisted they could hear Lincoln's boots pacing back and forth on the second floor. Truman told Lieber the story of how during the war he had on two occasions been woken in the night by a rapping on his bedroom door. Each time he thought it was somebody to tell him that Winston Churchill was telephoning from London. But when he opened the door no one was there.

Mrs Roosevelt told Lieber about a member of her staff who had seen an 'apparition' of Lincoln seated on his bed pulling on his boots, while a man who was Roosevelt's personal valet and houseman for eleven years revealed: 'The night before F.D.R.'s mother died there was such a scuffle of footsteps in the Blue Room that Harry Hopkins got annoyed. He told me to go in and see who was making all the noise. It wasn't anybody.' Furthermore, an important White House guest told Roosevelt she fainted after opening her bedroom door to a knock and seeing the 'Great Emancipator' standing there.

Katurah Brooks, a White House employee from 1931 to 1938, once told of how while working late in the Rose Room—no one else was on the second floor—she heard a sudden burst of laughter, 'loud and booming, like out of a cavern,' coming from the old Andrew Jackson bed.

Finally, the memoirs of Ike Hoover, Chief Usher of the White House for over forty years, 'abound with spectres,' according to Lieber. Besides the spirit forms of Lincoln and Andrew Jackson, those of Ulysses S. Grant, William Henry Harrison, who died in the White House, and Abigail Adams, wife of the second President, have been seen, it is claimed.

'Coming Events . . .'

IS IT POSSIBLE for a man, no matter what his station in life, to foresee his death? To have a dream, a vision, a warning, one that is so chillingly accurate he is left in no doubt about his fate? Yes, as countless cases throughout the world prove, it is. One of the most astonishing and evidential concerns Abraham Lincoln for as his own words show he saw his assassination in a terrifyingly accurate dream preview.

It came but a few days before the fateful night of 14th April, 1865, when he was slain. The President told a small group of people, which included his wife, of a disturbing and tragic dream he had experienced. One of those present, Ward Lamon, described the impressive scene when Mrs Lincoln, perturbed by the expression on her husband's face, asked, 'What is the matter?'

'I am afraid that I have done wrong to mention the subject at all,' he said, 'but somehow the thing has got possession of me and, like Banquo's ghost, it will not lie down.' Mrs Lincoln urged her husband to tell the dream, and was seconded by another listener. Lincoln hesitated, but at length began, very deliberately, his brow overcast with a shade of melancholy.

'I retired very late,' he said. 'I had been waiting up for important dispatches from the front. I could not have been long in bed when I fell into a slumber, for I was very weary. I soon began to dream. There seemed to be a death-like stillness about me.

'Then I heard subdued sobs, as if a number of people were weeping. I thought I left my bed and wandered downstairs. There the silence was broken by the same pitiful weeping, but the mourners were invisible. I went from room to room. No living person was in sight, but the same mournful sounds of distress met me as I passed along. It was light in all the rooms, every object was familiar to me. But where were all the people who were grieving as though their hearts would break?

'Determined to find the cause of a state of things so mysterious and so shocking, I kept on until I arrived at the East Room, which I entered. There I met with a sickening surprise.

'Before me was a catafalque, on which rested a corpse wrapped in funeral vestments. Around it were stationed soldiers who were acting as guards. There was a throng of people, some gazing mournfully upon the corpse, whose face was covered, others weeping pitifully. Who is dead in the White House? I asked one of the soldiers. "The President," was his answer. "He was killed by an assassin!"'

A few days later, this scene, precisely as it was described by Lincoln, was tragically enacted in all its details in the East Room of the White House, while the streets of an entire nation were draped in deepest mourning.

There is proof aplenty to show that Lincoln was not only deeply fascinated and absorbed by mediums, Spiritualism and seances, but that sittings were regularly held in the White House. Direct testimony came from Colonel S. P. Kase, of Philadelphia, a millionaire railroad builder who became a friend of the President.

Kase was present at a seance given by Mrs M. E. Williams. She suggested to Kase that he should leave some personal record of the President's psychic sessions, many of which were held during the troubled, turbulent times of the Civil War. The Colonel did—and even claimed that Lincoln's move to abolish slavery was as a direct result of spirit guidance. Here, in his own words, is his testimony:

'I believe that President Lincoln was induced, by the knowledge received through Spiritualism, to issue his famous Proclamation of Emancipation. My knowledge on that subject is extensive. I had occasion to visit Washington in 1862 on railroad business. Arriving early in the afternoon, I took a walk down Pennsylvania Avenue to the Capitol grounds. Passing a house near the grounds where I had formerly boarded I saw the name of H. Conkling on the door . . . I knew Conkling to be a writing medium. As I looked at the house, a voice alongside of me said: "Go in and see him. He is in the same room you used to occupy."

'I had no power,' said Col Kase, 'to move forward. I felt that I must enter the house, and I did. As I entered the room, Conkling was sitting in a corner and was in the act of sealing a letter. He at once said: "Mr Kase, I want you to carry this letter to the President. You can see him but I cannot." I observed, "I cannot take your letter, send it by mail." He said, "you must take it to him, otherwise he will not see it."

'I replied, "I can't take your letter as I am not acquainted with the President and I am on important business and want to be introduced to him under different auspices than delivering a letter I know nothing about."

'Immediately the voice behind me said, "Go, see what will become of this." It was the same voice that I had heard upon the street. My mind changed instantly. I said: "I will go if you will go along too. Give me the letter." Conkling said: "I cannot see him, but you can." All this time Conkling remained in an abnormal state. We arrived at the White House about dusk. I rang the bell and a servant opened the door. The President was at tea, but would see me after that.

'When we had entered the parlour Conkling said: "I cannot see him, but you can." Presently the servant came to the door and invited me forward. He opened the door of the President's room. The President was coming forward to meet me. I remarked: "This is the President. Mr Lincoln, I presume." He hesitated but finally said, "Yes." I said, "My name is S. P. Kase, of Danville, Pennsylvania." "Oh," he remarked, "you are from Pennsylvania. Be seated." I took a chair on one side of the table; he on the other.

'I handed him the Conkling letter, and after reading it he looked at me and said, "What does this mean?" I answered, "I do not know, Mr President, but I presume it means just what it says." He again read it over to himself very carefully and said again, "What can this mean?" I reiterated what I had said. "You think it means what it says, but you do not know its contents?" he said, to which I smilingly said I thought so.

'"Well, Sir," he observed, "I will read it to you"—which he did. The letter read: "I have been sent from the City of New York by spiritual influences to confer with you pertaining to the interest of the nation. I cannot return until I have an interview. Please appoint the time. Yours etc, H. B. Conkling."'

During the next four weeks Kase did his own business and was standing in the gallery of the Congress Hall, well satisfied with the results of his mission, when an old lady approached him handing him a card saying, 'Call any time it will suit you.' This was Mrs Laurie, a Spiritualist of Georgetown.

With his friend, Judge Wattles, he called that night about 8.00 p.m.

and there found the President and Mrs Lincoln. Soon he observed a young girl walking towards the President from the other end of the large parlour. Her eyes were closed. She came to the President and said: 'Sir, you were called to the position you occupy for a very great purpose. The world is universally in bondage. It must be physically set free, so that it may mentally rise to its proper status. There is a spiritual congress supervising the affairs of this nation as well as a congress at Washington. This republic will lead the van of republics throughout the world.'

'This was the text,' said Colonel Kase, 'on which she lectured the President for a full hour and a half, dwelling strongly on the importance of the emancipation of the slaves.' Among other things, she prophesied that from the time of the issuing of the Emancipation Proclamation there would be no reverses to the Union armies. 'I never listened,' he said, 'to a lecture so grand and sublime, so full of thought as this— delivered by a little girl who must have been under deep control of the spirit of some ancient philosopher.' Within some three or four weeks after these manifestations in interviews, President Lincoln issued his Emancipation Proclamation, to take effect on 1st January, 1863.

But who was the 'young girl' who so captivated the President with her trance spirit utterances? Who was Mrs Laurie? Research shows the medium was Nettie Colburn Maynard, who frequently visited the White House from 1863 until 1865. There is sufficient independently available material to prove this as fact, not mere fallacy. Indeed, some witnesses to the seances even swore affidavits to that effect.

It was in Georgetown that Miss Maynard first came into contact with the Lincolns. Luckily for us, she left a wealth of material concerning her visits to the President.

The medium was 'astonished' on her arrival at Georgetown to be presented to Mrs Lincoln. Also present were a man named Newton, Secretary of the Interior Department, the Rev John Pierpoint, at that time one of the chief clerks in the Treasury Building, and the Hon D. E. Somes, ex-member of the Congress from Biddeford, Maine. Mrs Lincoln told Nettie she had heard about another medium, Belle Miller, whose father was Cranston Laurie, for many years statistician of the Post Office Department.

'She had expressed a desire to see a trance medium,' Nettie recorded, 'when they had told her of myself. Fearing that I was already on my way to Baltimore with my brother, as I expected to leave that morning, she had said at once, "Perhaps they have not gone; suppose you take the carriage and ascertain." ' Nettie was entranced for one hour. We do not know what, or who, spoke through her lips. But it had a devastating effect on Mrs Lincoln.

'This young lady must not leave Washington,' she stated. 'I feel she must stay here and Mr Lincoln must hear what we have heard. It is all-important and he must hear it.' Nettie explained that her livelihood depended mainly on her effort as a speaker; there was no suitable opening in Washington. 'There are other things you can do,' Mrs Lincoln replied. 'Surely young ladies get excellent pay in the different departments. You can have a position in one of them, I am sure.' Here Mr Newton entered the conversation and promised to find young Nettie employment within his department. He did. It was settled. The medium stayed in Washington.

In December 1862 Mrs Laurie received a letter inviting her to the White House. There was a telling request. Nettie, too, was to attend. Later she recalled her first meeting with Lincoln, stating: 'I felt all the natural trepidation of a young girl about to enter the presence of the highest magistrate in our land; being fully impressed with the dignity of his office, and feeling that I was about to meet some superior being; and it was almost with trembling that I entered with my friends the Red Parlour of the White House, at eight o'clock that evening.

'Mrs Lincoln received us graciously, and introduced us to a gentleman and lady present whose names I have forgotten. Mr Lincoln was not then present. While all were conversing pleasantly on general subjects, Mrs Miller seated herself, under control, at the double grand piano at one side of the room, seemingly awaiting someone. Mrs Lincoln was talking with us in a pleasant strain when suddenly Mrs Miller's hand fell upon the keys with a force that betokened a master hand, and the strains of a grand march filled the room. As the measured notes rose and fell we became silent. The heavy end of the piano began rising and falling in perfect time to the music. All at once it ceased, and Mr Lincoln stood upon the threshold of the room. He afterwards informed us that the first notes of the music fell upon his ears as he reached the head of the grand staircase to descend, and that he kept step to the music until he reached the doorway.

'Mr and Mrs Laurie and Mrs Miller were duly presented. Then I was led forward and presented. He stood before me, tall and kindly, with a smile on his face. Dropping his hand upon my head, he said, in a humorous tone, "So this is our 'little Nettie' is it, that we have heard so much about?" I could only smile and say, "Yes, sir," like any school girl; when he kindly led me to an ottoman. Sitting down in a chair, the ottoman at his feet, he began asking me questions in a kindly way about my mediumship; and I think he must have thought me stupid, as my answers were little beyond a "Yes" and "No." His manner, however, was genial and kind, and it was then suggested we form in a circle. He said, "Well, how do you do it?" looking at me. Mr Laurie came to the rescue, and said we had been accustomed to sit in a circle and join hands; but he did not think it would be necessary in this instance. While he was speaking, I lost all consciousness of my surroundings and passed under control.

'For more than an hour I was made to talk to him, and I learned from my friends afterwards that it was upon matters that he seemed fully to understand, while they comprehended very little until that portion was reached that related to the forthcoming Emancipation Proclamation. He was charged with the utmost solemnity and force of manner not to abate the terms of its issue, and not to delay its enforcement as a law beyond the opening of the year; and he was assured that it was to be the crowning event of his administration and his life; and that while he was being counselled by strong parties to defer the enforcement of it, hoping to supplant it by other measures and to delay action, he must in no wise heed such counsel, but stand firm to his convictions and fearlessly perform the work and fulfil the mission for which he had been raised up by an over-ruling Providence. Those present declared that they lost sight of the timid girl in the majesty of the utterance, the strength and force of the language, and the importance of that which was conveyed, and seemed to realise that some strong masculine spirit force was giving speech to almost divine commands.

'I shall never forget the scene around me when I regained consciousness. I was standing in front of Mr Lincoln, and he was sitting back in his chair, with his arms folded upon his breast looking intently at me. I stepped back, naturally confused at the situation—not remembering at once where I was; and glancing around the group, where perfect silence reigned. It took me a moment to remember my whereabouts. A gentleman present then said in a low tone, "Mr President, did you notice anything peculiar in the method of address?" Mr Lincoln raised himself, as if shaking off his spell. He glanced quickly at the full-length portrait of Daniel Webster, that hung above the piano, and replied. "Yes, and it is very singular, very!" with a marked emphasis.

'Mr Somes said: "Mr President, would it be improper for me to inquire whether there has been any pressure brought to bear upon you to defer the enforcement of the Proclamation?" To which the President replied: "Under these circumstances that question is perfectly proper, as we are all friends (smiling upon the company). It is taking all my nerve and strength to withstand such a pressure." At this point the gentlemen drew around him, and spoke together in low tones, Mr Lincoln saying least of all. At last he turned to me, and laying his hand upon my head, uttered these words in a manner that I shall never forget: "My child, you possess a very singular gift; but that it is of God, I have no doubt. I thank you for coming here tonight. It is more important than perhaps any one present can understand. I must leave you all now; but I hope I shall see you again." He shook me kindly by the hand, bowed to the rest of the company, and was gone. We remained an hour longer, talking with Mrs Lincoln and her friends, and then returned to Georgetown. Such was my first interview with Abraham Lincoln, and the memory of it is as clear and vivid as the evening on which it occurred.'

Subsequently, Nettie demonstrated her mediumship to a host of influential Washington people. At the home of Joshua Speed, Lincoln's former law partner, 'I gave many private sittings to distinguished people whose names I never knew.'

In early February 1863, a note was received from Mrs Lincoln inviting Nettie and others for a seance that night. Before the party left Nettie went into trance. Her guide said the President would be present. Mr Laurie thought this unlikely. Lincoln, he stated, would hardly leave the White House to attend a seance. But he did.

Here, again in Nettie's words, is what transpired:

'However, when the bell rang, Mr Laurie, in honour of his expected guest, went to the door to receive them in person. His astonishment was great to find Mr Lincoln standing on the threshold, wrapped in his long cloak; and to hear his cordial "Good evening," as he put out his hand and entered. Mr Laurie promptly exclaimed, "Welcome, Mr Lincoln, to my humble roof; you were expected." Mr Lincoln stopped in the act of removing his cloak and said, "Expected! Why, it is only five minutes since I knew that I was coming." He came down from a cabinet meeting as Mrs Lincoln and her friends were about to enter the carriage, and asked them where they were going. She replied, "To Georgetown; to a circle." He answered immediately, "Hold on a moment, I will go with you." "Yes," said Mrs Lincoln, "and I was never so surprised in my life." He seemed pleased when Mr Laurie explained the source of our information; and I think it had a tendency to prepare his mind to receive what followed, and to obey the instructions given. On this occasion, as he entered the parlour, I made bold to say to him, "I would like to speak a word with you, Mr Lincoln, before you go, after the circle." "Certainly," he said, "remind me, should I forget it."

'Mr and Mrs Laurie, with their daughter, Mrs Miller, at his request, sang several fine old Scotch airs—among them one that he declared a favourite, called Bonnie Doon. I can see him now, as he sat in the old high-backed rocking-chair; one leg thrown over the arm; leaning back in utter weariness, with his eyes closed, listening to the low, strong, and clear yet plaintive notes, rendered as only the Scots can sing their native melodies. I looked at his face, and it appeared tired and haggard. He seemed older by years than when I had seen him a few weeks previously. The whole party seemed anxious and troubled; but all interest centred in the chief, and all eyes and thoughts were turned on him.

'At the end of the song he turned to me and said, "Well, Miss Nettie; do you think you have anything to say to me tonight?" At first I thought he referred to the request I had made when he entered the room. Recollecting myself, however, I said, "If I have not, there may be others who have." He nodded his head in a pleasant manner, saying, "Suppose we see what they will have to tell us."

'Among the spirit friends that have ever controlled me since my first development, was one known as "old Dr Bamford." He was quite a favourite with Mr Lincoln. His quaint dialect, old-fashioned methods of expression, straightforwardness in arriving at his subject, together with fearlessness of utterance, recommended him as no finished style could have done. This spirit took possession of me at once. As I learned from those in the circle, the substance of his remarks was as follows: "That a very precarious state of things existed at the front, where General Hooker had just taken command. The army was totally demoralised; regiments stacking arms, refusing to obey orders or to do duty; threatening a general retreat; declaring their purpose to return to Washington." A vivid picture was drawn of the terrible state of affairs, greatly to the surprise of all present, save the chief to whom the words were addressed.

'When the picture had been painted in vivid colours, Mr Lincoln quietly remarked; "You seem to understand the situation. Can you point out the remedy?" Dr Bamford immediately replied: "Yes, if you have the courage to use it." He smiled, they said, and answered, "Try me." The old doctor then said to him, "It is one of the simplest, and being so simple it may not appeal to you as being sufficient to cope with what threatens to prove a serious difficulty. The remedy lies with yourself.

'"Go in person to the front; taking with you your wife and children; leaving behind your official dignity, and all manner of display. Resist the importunities of officials to accompany you, and take only such attendants as may be absolutely necessary; avoid the high grade officers, and seek the tents of the private soldiers. Inquire into their grievances; show yourself to be what you are, The Father of your People. Make them feel that you are interested in their sufferings, and that you are not unmindful of the many trials which beset them in their march through the dismal swamps, whereby both their courage and numbers have been depleted."

'He quietly remarked, "If that will do any good, it is easily done." The doctor instantly replied: "It will do all that is required. It will unite the soldiers as one man. It will unite them to you in bands of steel. And now, if you would prevent a serious, if not fatal, disaster to your cause, let the news be promulgated at once, and disseminated throughout the camp of the Army of the Potomac. Have it scattered broadcast that you are on the eve of visiting the front; that you are not talking of it, but that it is settled that you are going, and are now getting into readiness. This will stop insubordination and hold the soldiers in check; being something to divert their minds, and they will wait to see what your coming portends." He at once said, "It shall be done."

'A long conversation then followed between the doctor and Mr Lincoln regarding the state of affairs, and the war generally. The old doctor told him that he would be renominated and re-elected to the Presidency. They said that he sadly smiled when this was told him, saying, "It is hardly an honour to be coveted, save one could find it his duty to accept it." After the circle was over, Mr Laurie said, "Mr Lincoln, it is possible that affairs are as bad as has been depicted?" He said, "They can hardly be exaggerated; but I ask it as a favour of all present that they do not speak of these things. The major there," pointing to an officer of that rank who was in their party, "has just brought despatches from the front depicting the state of affairs pretty much as our old friend has shown it; and we were just having a Cabinet meeting regarding the matter, when something, I know not what, induced me to leave the room and come downstairs, when I found Mrs Lincoln in the act of coming here. I felt it might be of service for me to come; I did not know wherefore." He dropped his head as he said this—leaning forward in his chair as if he were thinking aloud. Then looking up suddenly, he remarked, "Matters are pretty serious down there, and perhaps the simplest remedy is the best. I have often noticed in life that little things have sometimes greater weight than larger ones." '

What did Lincoln make of these and other seances? When this point was put to him by Mr Somes, the President replied: "I am not prepared to describe the intelligence that controls this young girl's organism. She certainly could have no knowledge of the facts communicated to me, nor of what was transpiring in my Cabinet meeting prior to my joining this circle, nor of affairs at the front (the army), nor regarding transpiring events which are known to me only, and which I have not imparted to any one, and which have not been made public." How delighted Nettie must have been when the President followed her advice. The next day it was reported that Lincoln planned to visit the Army of the Potomac. This, said Nettie, 'and other matter,' showed 'liberal obedience to the directions given the previous night.'

During a two-month period Nettie gave a number of seances to President and Mrs Lincoln. 'These,' said the medium, 'took place by appointment. At the close of one, Mrs Lincoln would make an appointment engaging me to come at a certain hour of the day, which usually would be in the vicinity of one o'clock, the time when Mr Lincoln usually partook of his luncheon.'

To return to Lincoln's previews, it is also germain to add that before America's slaves were freed, the President had several strange dreams. Lincoln saw a series of angels. When he asked who they were, they replied: 'We are such as come in God's name for freedom's sake. Behold millions of his angels come down from heaven and would come to thy armies, if thou wouldst proclaim freedom of the slaves.'

Lincoln woke much troubled with the dream. The next night the 'angels' came again, repeated their words, and added: 'The great majority of the country is ripe for this matter. Thou fearest this is but a foolish dream. Behold, we will give thee proof tomorrow. God is in this matter. Save thou proclaimest the freedom of the slaves, thou shalt not succeed. Do thou this, and the enemy's armies shall melt away like snow in the sun.'

That Lincoln had nocturnal visions there is no doubt. Neither is there doubt that he knew his days were numbered, that soon he would enter the world whence Nettie Maynard's communicators came . . .

Famed—and Infamous

THERE ARE CERTAIN figures in history who because of their fame—or more probably their infamy—have a reputation far beyond the confines of their own country. Examples readily spring to mind. Joan of Arc is one, Abraham Lincoln another. Into this category easily fits a third character, but one of disrepute, Rasputin, the mysterious so-called mad monk who exhibited a Svengali-like hold over some members of the Imperial Russian Royal Family.

'All my life I have been defending my father,' said his daughter, then aged seventy-six and living in Los Angeles. 'He was,' she said, 'an exceptional man with psychic powers, who was misunderstood.'

Some years ago a letter by Czar Nicholas II, describing the first audience given to Rasputin, was auctioned at Sotheby's. Dated 16th October, 1906 it is addressed to Peter Stolypin, Council of Ministers president.

'I received a peasant from the government of Tobolsk, Grigori Rasputin,' it reads. 'He brought me an icon of St Simeon. He made a remarkably strong impression both on Her Majesty and myself, so that our conversation lasted for more than an hour. He would very much like to see you and bless you daughter with the icon.'

Though Rasputin was unable to help Stolypin's daughter, whose feet had been smashed in a bomb explosion two months earlier, his influence over these aristocrats grew. In the case of the Tsarina, it reached hypnotic proportions.

The story of Rasputin's sense of mission begins at the age of twelve. He and his brother were bathing in a river when the latter got out of his depth. Rasputin tried to save him, but the boy drowned. This made Rasputin believe he had himself been preserved for a special reason.

In his teens, he married a peasant girl. Their child died within six months. In misery, Rasputin consulted a local 'holy man' named Makari who told him: 'Do not grieve. God has marked you out for one of His own.'

The years passed. A vision of the Virgin Mary which appeared to Rasputin one day was interpreted by Makari thus, 'You will become a holy man.'

Rasputin was never a monk, as he has been dubbed. He became a wandering pilgrim and joined a sect who taught him healing techniques and the gift of prophecy. His long hair, piercing gaze and persuasive voice compelled the attention of crowds he addressed. His reputation for healing grew. Meeting with Church dignitaries led to the Imperial Palace visit described in the letter to Stolypin.

The Tsarina had prayed fervently for a son and heir. At birth, Alexis was found to be suffering from hemophilia. Whenever he bled, 'no aid short of the miraculous could staunch the blood.'

Rasputin was called in when doctors failed. It was Alexis's second birthday; he had injured his leg. As Rasputin touched it the bleeding stopped. Turning to the parents he said, 'Do not be alarmed, you son will live and the disease will disappear.' The healing was never officially announced but rumours spread.

Some years ago Igor Vinogradoff, of Sotheby's book department, was able to throw some light on Rasputin.

'I knew Stolypin's daughter in later life,' he explained. 'She was an intelligent child of twelve when Rasputin saw her. She was not impressed by him. If he blessed her, it may have helped her to recover, though she had no feet.

'Very few people ever saw Rasputin. The Empress kept him to herself and her family. He was the last hope for the boy. When Rasputin died, he was found to have seven bank accounts. He took money from everyone. He was always writing to Government Ministers urging them to offer work to certain contractors. Often he wrote notes on behalf of people competing for the same contract, getting a large fee from each. It was a sort of confidence trick.'

Of his first meeting with Rasputin, Prince Yussoupov, who helped murder the so-called starets—a man of God—wrote:

'The "starets" made me lie down on the sofa. Then, staring intently at me, he gently ran his hand over my chest, neck and head, after which he knelt down, laid both hands on my forehead and murmured a prayer. His face was so close to mine that I could see only his eyes. He remained in this position for some time, then rising brusquely, he made mesmeric passes over my body.

'Rasputin had tremendous hypnotic power. I felt as if some active energy were pouring heat, like a warm current, into my whole being. I fell into a torpor, and my body grew numb. I tried to speak but my tongue no longer obeyed me and I gradually slipped into a drowsy state, as though a powerful narcotic had been administered to me. All I could see was Rasputin's glittering eyes; two phosphorescent beams of light melting into a great luminous ring which at times drew nearer and then moved farther away. I heard the voice of the starets, but could not understand what he said.

'I remained in this state without being able to cry out or to move. My mind alone was free and I fully realised I was gradually falling into the power of this evil man. Then I felt stir in me the will to fight his hypnosis. Little by little the desire to resist grew stronger and stronger, forming a protective armour around me. I had the feeling that a merciless struggle was being fought out between Rasputin and me. I knew that I was preventing him from getting complete mastery over me, but still I could not move. I had to wait until he ordered me to get up.'

Born Gregori Efimovich, the son of a farmer who was once a coachman in the Imperial Mail, Rasputin was thirty-three when he first met the Imperial Family and forty-four when he died. In December 1916, Rasputin wrote a letter which shows clearly he 'knew' his time on earth was running short.

'I feel that I shall leave life before 1st January,' he said. 'I wish to make it known to the Russian people . . . to the Russian Mother and the Children, to the land of Russsia what they must understand.

'If I am killed by common assassins, and especially by my brothers the Russian peasants, you, Czar of Russia, have nothing to fear, remain on your throne and govern, and you, Russian Czar, will have nothing to fear for your children. They will reign for hundreds of years in Russia. But if I am murdered by nobles, and if they shed my blood, their hands will remain soiled with my blood . . .

'They will leave Russia. Brothers will kill brothers, and they will kill each other and hate each other, and for twenty-five years there will be no nobles in the country. Czar of the land of Russia, if you hear the sound of the bell which will tell you that Gregori has been killed, you must know this: if it was your relations who have wrought my death then no one of your family, that is to say, none of your children or relations, will remain alive for more than two years. They will be killed by the Russian people . . . I shall be killed. I am no longer among the living. Pray, pray, be strong. Think of your blessed family.'

And the Royal Family was involved in Rasputin's death for it was Prince Yussoupov who first offered him poisoned cakes. At first refusing, Rasputin changed his mind and ate two. Nothing happened. Next Rasputin drank two glasses of laced Madeira. Again, nothing happened. Yussoupov fired the first shot into Rasputin. That, too, failed to kill him. All told it took five bullets to inflict death. Four were delivered by a fellow conspirator.

Three days later, on 1st January, 1917 Rasputin's body was found. Rolled up in a blue curtain, tied with rope, it had been pushed through a hole in the frozen River Neva. Two days later, Rasputin was buried in a corner of the Imperial Park. Before the coffin lid was sealed, the Empress had two objects put on Rasputin's breast. The first was an icon, which bore the signatures of herself, her husband, her son and daughters. The other was a letter which pleaded: 'My dear martyr. Give me thy blessing that it may follow me always on the sad and dreary path I have yet to follow here below. And remember us from on high in your holy prayers. Alexandra.'

Even in his violent death, Russia's most powerful woman sought guidance, help and reassurance in her life. That, as Rasputin had predicted, was running out. Alexandra was killed by a single bullet following the Russian Revolution. Her husband died instantly. Alexandra had time for one final act. She raised her hand and made the sign of the cross.

Concerning Communist rulers, of all the grim-faced, sombre, men to have lived within the Kremlin's walls, one of the most feared was without doubt Stalin. His ruthless Communism and purges are estimated to have cost millions their lives. Yet even he knew something about psychic gifts. In fact, so impressed was he by one, a certain Wolf Messing, that the psychic was given permission to tour freely throughout Russia.

But that was not until Messing personally proved his ability to Stalin. Now, though Russia as a State teaches that death is the end, that humans do not survive beyond the grave, none other than Kruschev, the man once so feared by the West—and no more so than during the Cuban missile crisis—saw a ghost.

Good authority has it that returning to his seat during a performance at the Moscow Arts Theatre he encountered in a corridor the unmistakable phantom of Nicholas II, the last Czar of Russia who was shot by the Bolsheviks in 1918. Apparently, Kruschev was so shaken by the sight of the spectre that he was visibly ill for several days afterwards.

However, some at least will have disagreed with the Soviet leader's remark passed in 1963 when in East Berlin he announced that Russia had a 100-megaton bomb which could kill 700-800 million people. 'It is not advisable to be in a hurry for the other world,' he grunted. 'Nobody ever returned from there to report that one lives better there than here.' Six years earlier, during an interview with an American correspondent, Kruschev announced, 'We are atheists.' To this he added: 'How can we understand it when churchmen, clergymen, throw holy water on guns if they are intended to kill people? Is that the highest showing of man's spirit.'

Later he referred to what he termed 'the colonialists' who came with armies, brought the Church and God with them and killed defenceless people in peaceful lands. 'They brought the cross and the bible,' he continued. 'They left the people with religion and took all the people had.'

In recent years Russia has undoubtedly spent millions upon millions of roubles on psychic research. There is evidence too that before his death Soviet President Leonid Brezhnev was treated by a psychic healer, Djourna Davitachvili. Journalist Henry Gris, an expert on supernormal research behind the Iron Curtain, went to Russia and collected evidence to back this astonishing claim.

It was reported that when former West German Chancellor Schmidt met Brezhnev at the Kremlin, he noted that the President had been cured of his ailments.

When Brezhnev took one winter holiday the seventy-three year-old Soviet leader had slurred speech and an unsteady walk. Soon he had renewed vigour in bearing, face and voice.

The 'elegant' Djourna was summoned, some say, to heal him after curing other high-ranking officials of various diseases by simple hand passes.

She interprets her gift as an ability to transmit a stream of 'bio-energy' from the palms of her hands. Djourna maintains that everyone has this energy field, but hers is somehow stronger and capable of triggering sufficient power to cure certain diseases.

A natural psychic who has been aware of her gifts since childhood, she then saw rainbow-like light above flowers and trees. She also heard sounds as if each tree was an orchestra and every flower a singer. Patient's auras are visible to her.

Gris took photographs of Djourna at work in a clinic. He saw her treat thirteen patients with spinal disorders, and diagnose a stomach ulcer for one woman which was later confirmed by doctors.

Former waitress Djourna who, as far as I know still lives in Georgia, would go to Moscow to treat patients at her apartment, hospitals and clinics.

The Russian newspaper *Trud* published an interview with a Soviet Academy of Science member, Alexander Spirkin, who has documented Djourna's gift and those of other sensitives.

This scientist asked Djourna to treat an ulcer. After fifteen minutes' healing the bandages were removed from the patient. The ulcer had dried completely. Five minutes after that a light pink film appeared, 'evidencing the formation of skin cells.'

The French newspaper *Nice Matin* reported that Soviet scientists refer to Djourna as 'extra-sensitive with high biological energy.' Her successes have prompted intensive research to be undertaken into 'extra-sensitives' at Moscow's Academy of Science.

Meanwhile, the Communist youth paper *Komsomolskaya Pravda* said Djourna's gift was not in conflict with official medicine and that she worked in co-operation with doctors. An accompanying commentary in the same paper came from Y. Kobzaryov, a member of the Soviet Academy of Science. He said that these phenomena were real and not mystical. There had always been, as there still were, people who healed by laying on of hands.

In his view the results could not be explained away by suggestion or hypnosis. Enough was known to show that some healers emanated electro-magnetic waves. These could burn the skin. It might be that they had a physical rather than a psychological effect on the patient's organism.

Kobzaryov pointed out there had been a long Soviet fascination for parapsychology. 'We still know next to nothing about these physical fields and the role they play,' he declared. 'The importance of further research into these fields can hardly be overestimated.'

Djourna, officially recognised by her government was, it is said, granted the freedom of shopping sorties to both Paris and London. At her native town of Tbilisi, the healer had two homes, three cars, a maid, a cook and chauffeur.

Djourna has no idea how her healing gift works, only that it does and that it takes practically no effort on her part. As far as Djourna is concerned 'there are no good people and bad people, only those who are sick.'

Gris was the first Western journalist allowed to meet the healer, who, according to one West German magazine, was 'the female Rasputin of the Kremlin.' In one report, Gris said Djourna, known as Comrade D, had the 'hard men of the Kremlin' at her feet. Her healing gifts 'have won her fame and the sort of VIP treatment normally reserved for top ballerinas and senior Party officials.'

Djourna was summoned to Brezhnev after curing other high-ranking officials of various diseases simply by touching them. Soviet Prime Minister Kosygin is also believed to have been helped by the healer. She claims to have cured thousands of others, whose ailments included ulcers, heart disease and some types of cancer. An official warned Gris, 'You are not to ask if she has been treating Brezhnev or Kosygin even though all Moscow knows she has.' He saw six bodyguards flank Djourna as she came down the marble staircase from her de luxe suite at a Moscow hotel. In contrast to the normal drab Soviet clothes, she wore a black suede, fur-trimmed coat and black trouser suit. An armed guard saluted Djourna as she passed a crowd hoping to see her. She climbed into a black limousine with Gris to begin her 'tour of duty.'

Djourna, it is believed, saw the Russian President daily at his flat and treated him for one minute.

'I believe,' said Gris, 'she was allowed to speak to me to let Western leaders know they had better think again if they are hoping ill-health will force Brezhnev to quit.'

The healer's first stop was to address a meeting of cancer experts. One of them, Dr Yanis Lacis, confirmed that a patient's orange-sized tumour dissolved after twenty minutes' healing. Then came other appointments, diagnoses at home and medics' offices, consultations and treatments of the bedridden.

At Moscow Hospital No 68, Dr Ruben Davidov testified to the recovery of a 'lost cause,' an eighteen-year-old patient suffering from ulcers.

Djourna's success, said Gris, 'has brought her rewards incredible by

Soviet standards.' She is one of Russia's richest women, charging up to £150 a session.

When she was two, 'my father made me press my heels on the small of his back to cure his sciatica,' said Djourna. 'It was a skill in my family that went back for generations.'

Even as a child neighbours sought her healing. 'I learned to help them by seeking out the sources of their pain with the palm of my hand.'

Djourna keeps her palm over the affected area. What Soviet scientists call 'bio-energy' leaves her palm. 'So,' said Djourna, 'the healing begins. Don't ask me why. It takes practically no effort on my part.' Then, Gris ended, she swept off to her luxury hotel and crowds of waiting admirers.

Lev Kolodnyi, the Communist youth paper reporter, saw Djourna revive a bouquet of dried roses by passing her hands over them, and perform other wonders. He asked for the formation of a scientific centre to study such phenomena. According to a previous report a laboratory was specially founded to investigate her healing ability.

Djourna is also credited with successful healing of other high officials. Two have been named, Nikolai Baibakov, Minister of Planning, and Boris Petrovsky, Minister of Health. Kolodnyi said that Djourna was not in conflict with official medicine. She worked in co-operation with doctors.

In her apartment Djourna led Kolódnyi to a bowl of roses that were closed and had lost their scent. She bent over the flowers and pressed her hands over them. 'Immediately,' said the reporter, 'a scent of roses flowed towards me as though Djourna had opened a bottle of perfume. Then one after the other, the rose petals began opening up.'

Delighted with this effect, Djourna sat down and placed her fingers over an empty cardboard cigarette box. She 'raised her hand and the box rose with it.' Then she told Kolodnyi: 'There is a yellow and blue light over your head. I think you have a headache.' This was correct. He had not slept much the previous night and had got up early. Djourna placed her hands lightly over his head. He felt a faint breeze, and the pain stopped.

Additionally, another Russian publication, *Little Flame*, a weekly magazine of pictures and popular articles, said the healer's claims should not be dismissed without serious study. Cited was evidence from tests in a state clinic which produced measurable improvements in patients Djourna treated.

To turn the clock back a few years earlier, psychic Wolf Messing literally came face to face with Stalin, convinced him of his powers and unlike even ordinary folk was allowed to travel freely within the USSR. Messing certainly had a dramatic introduction to Stalin, the Great Dictator.

In the middle of a packed Russian theatre where he was demonstrating his gifts, two hard-faced Soviet policemen suddenly appeared unannounced and uninvited on to the stage. They told the audience in the city of Gomel, 'We are sorry but the show is over.' They hustled Messing into a car and drove him to an unknown destination.

The psychic was worried. This was 1940 when people were carted away by police with no questions asked or reasons given and vanished for ever. Messing asked about his hotel bill and trunk. The police said the trunk would not be needed. The hotel bill was settled. When they arrived at a town that was strange to the psychic he was led into a room which seemed to be part of a hotel. Presently he was taken to another room.

Then a man he speedily recognised came in. It was Stalin. What he sought from Messing was information about some of his influential Polish friends. Would he tell Stalin the plans of these Polish leaders and what was happening in their country?

Messing, even in those war days, was a famous psychic who had travelled the world. He had demonstrated his gifts to people like Einstein, Freud, Gandhi and others in high places. His friends included Marshal Pilsudski, the Polish leader, and many in his government.

This first meeting with Stalin led to a series of strange but triumphantly successful encounters with the dictator. At one of them Stalin demanded a test. Messing was to pull off a 'psychic' bank robbery and obtain 100,000 roubles from the Moscow Gosbank where he was not known.

The psychic walked up to the cashier and handed him a blank piece of paper torn from a school notebook. Then he opened his attache case, which he put on the counter. Mentally he willed the cashier to hand over 100,000 roubles. The old cashier looked at the paper, opened his safe and removed 100,000 roubles. These notes were stuffed by Messing into his case. He left the bank joined by Stalin's two official witnesses to the experiment.

When they had confirmed Messing's success, the psychic returned to the cashier. As he handed over the package of bank notes, the cashier looked at the blank piece of paper on his desk and fell with a heart attack to the floor. Messing commented, 'Luckily it wasn't fatal.'

Stalin next demanded a more intriguing test. He arranged for the psychic to be taken to an important government office. Three different sets of guards were instructed not to allow Messing to leave the room or the building. He had no exit permit.

Messing, according to accounts, triumphed again. When he stepped outside the building he turned and waved to a high government official watching from a top-floor window of the room he had just left.

Both these claims were published in an important Russian journal, 'Science and Religion,' as part of Messing's autobiography. The fact that they passed both the political censors and the influential magazine's official atheistic policy is good evidence for their validity.

Another time Stalin asked Messing to obtain entry to his country dacha without an official pass or permission. The house was heavily guarded. Its staff members belonged to the secret police.

Again Messing triumphed. Asked how he did it, he replied that mentally he had suggested to guards and servants, 'I am Beria.' Beria, then head of Russia's secret police, was a constant visitor to this dacha. Messing did not resemble him in any way.

The result of Messing's successful tests imposed by Stalin led to the psychic receiving permission to tour freely through the entire Soviet Union.

The clairvoyant was able to demonstrate his psychic talents even during the most repressive years of Soviet rule. This was at a time when the government proclaimed telepathy did not exist and psychics were dismissed as rogues. Yet some of Messing's public engagements were made by the Ministry of Culture.

Messing escaped from the Nazis by crossing into Russia hidden in a wagonload of hay in November 1939. Yet three years later, as a private Soviet citizen, he bought and presented two fighter planes to Russia's Air Force. His name was written in large letters on the fuselages.

Messing, born a Jew, was a Polish immigrant. In a Warsaw theatre in 1937 he predicted to his 1,000 audience, 'Hitler will die if he turns to the East.' Hitler's army invaded Poland on 1st September, 1939. When news of Messing's prophecy reached Hitler he put a price of 200,000 marks on his head.

Messing told a fantastic story of his escape. On the day of the invasion he went into hiding in a Warsaw meat locker. Venturing into the street one night, he was siezed by a Nazi officer who identified him from a small booklet containing photographs of wanted people. After being assailed by the officer he was taken to a police station. There, Messing willed the police to gather in one room. This included the chief and sentry guarding the exit. Then quickly he left and reached the Russian border that night. The whole of his family were killed in the Warsaw Ghetto.

At his stage performances, Messing rarely deals with politics or personal matters. People in the audience are told to think of some task they would like him to perform. These are noted, sealed and delivered to a jury chosen by the audience.

Authors Sheila Ostrander and Lynn Schroeder described one of Messing's successes at a demonstration to medical people. The psychic walked slowly up and down the aisles. He paused at one row and chose a man in the fourth seat.

Then Messing reached into this man's pocket and removed scissors and a sponge. These he held up for the audience to see. 'I don't think I had better cut the sponge,' he said. Instead he took a piece of chalk and sketched the outline of a dog on the sponge. The jury confirmed that the request made by a volunteer was for Messing to find his friend and cut a dog's picture from the sponge in his pocket.

'People's thoughts come to me as pictures,' said Messing when in his seventies. He asserts that when blindfolded telepathy is easier for him.

Messing owes the discovery of his psychic powers to a curious happening when he worked as a messenger in Berlin. He fainted from hunger and was taken to hospital. Finding his body cold and no evidence of pulse or heart beats or breathing he was removed to the morgue. There a medical student chanced to note a very faint and almost undetectable heart beat. Three days later young Messing made a complete recovery.

In hospital he was examined by a Dr Abel, a psychiatrist and neuropathologist, who made him realise he was psychic. 'You have the ability of self-induced catalepsy as well as paranormal faculty,' he said.

With the help of a psychiatric colleague Abel helped Messing to develop his talent. A job was found for him in a Berlin waxworks. There he climbed into a crystal coffin, induced a state of catalepsy and lay like a corpse every week-end. His next job in a famous Berlin theatre was to play a fakir's role.

At sixteen Messing in Vienna was invited by Einstein to his flat. There he was introduced to Freud. They tested him. Freud mentally directed the young psychic to go to the bathroom cupboard, pick up some tweezers, return to Einstein and pull out three hairs from his moustache. The young Messing did precisely that.

During the next ten years he toured the world performing in many major capitals. In 1927 he met Gandhi in India. Again there was a test, this time a simple one. The mental request was for Messing to take a flute from the table and give it to a person in the room. He did so.

Perhaps it is worth adding that Stalin fleetingly referred to an afterlife during an interview with American journalist C. P. Nutter. He jokingly asked the Russian whether widespread rumours of his death were accurate. Doubtless pausing and puffing on his pipe, the leader answered: 'I know from foreign Press reports that I long ago abandoned this sinful world and moved into the other world. As one cannot doubt such reports unless he wants to be expelled from the list of civilised people, I request you to believe them and not disturb me in the calm of that other world.'

However, another American, an author, was not content to let Stalin rest, or otherwise, in the spirit world. Ruth Montgomery claimed that world-famous US medium Arthur Ford who died in 1971 returned to her every morning for five months for a fifteen-minute chat. In these talks she says he told her that Rudolph Valentino is now happily married in Paris and Stalin is reborn in Rhodesia.

It was claimed that other celebrities who have not been reborn still display interest in earthly affairs. Charles de Gaulle is watching Europe and the Middle East 'and is like a firehorse answering the call for his beloved France.'

Sir Winston Churchill and Franklin D. Roosevelt are described as the best of friends, absorbed in each other's politics. Napoleon reincarnated almost immediately, and saw life and death in the ranks as a lowly foot soldier.

Abraham Lincoln, said Miss Montgomery, is now in New Orleans where he is studying America's race problems. Meanwhile, John F. Kennedy is trying to arrange a settlement between Israelis and Arabs. His brother Bobby Kennedy is at work persuading civil rights leaders not to use violence.

To return to more factual accounts, proof exists that famous Victorian medium D. D. Home became a close friend of Czar

Alexander II. He it was who presented the medium with more than one precious jewel.

Home's Russian connection began when the much-travelled psychic celebrity visited Italy. Though ill, when in Rome he was presented to Countess de Koucheleff. The Countess invited Home to supper that night. There he met the Countesses sister, known as Sacha, otherwise Alexandra de Kroll. She was aged but seventeen. Seeing her for the very first time, Home received a strong psychic impression that 'she was to be my wife.' He was correct.

That the de Krol family were rich no one can deny. They moved in the best pre-Revolution social circles in St Petersburg. Alexandra was a god-daughter of a former Czar, Nicholas. The couple's wedding was to be held at Polonstrava, outside St Petersburg. This was one of the many estates owned by the de Koucheleff family, related by marriage to Alexandra.

Czar Alexander II listened with growing interest when he heard of Home's arrival within his country. Indeed, the Czar sent a message to the estate inviting the medium to an audience at the Winter Palace of St Petersburg. Home refused, saying his psychic gifts were not functioning. Undeterred, the Czar replied by saying he would like to meet Home as Mr Home, not as a medium. Again the invitation was rejected. Home explaired he had much to do with matters concerning his wedding.

Events then took a strange turn. Shortly before his marriage, Home's dead mother appeared to him at night. She advised her son to tell the Czar that his psychic powers had returned. Home complied with the spirit request. At once he received an invitation to spend not an evening but a whole week at the Winter Palace. This was the first of several visits to that palace and the Czar's summer residence at Tsarskoe-Selo.

Though no details are available of seance-room happenings at the Winter Palace, they were undoubtedly a success. Czar and psychic became close friends. The ruler intervened so that Home's marriage, which was threatened because of difficulties concerning the medium's personal papers, could go ahead. The medium and Alexandra were married in the August as planned. After Home left the Winter Palace, he was sent on the Czar's instructions a beautiful ring set with diamonds.

Later the medium again returned to Russia. The year was 1865. Revolution was a long way off. At the Czar's command the medium was lodged and attended on at one of the Imperial palaces. At his disposal were a carriage and horses.

Neither did official interest with Home end with the Czar. His brother, Grand Duke Constantine, invited him to his palace at Strelna. Unfortunately, the Czar had already summoned Home to the English Palace at Peterhoff. Here, Home wrote to a friend, several seances were held. Apparently, the Czar was well satisfied with the results.

Home's life was shattered when Alexandra died. Previously, when their child, Gregoire, was born, the Czar sent as a Christening gift a fabulous emerald surrounded by sixteen large diamonds. Alexandra died on 3rd July, 1862. Yet a further gift came from the Royal Russian when Home remarried in 1871. Alexander II gave the medium another magnificent ring which boasted a sapphire set in diamonds.

King of Clairvoyants

MANY COUNTRIES IN the world, because of past political or cultural links, have a special bond with Britain. Australia, America, India and New Zealand, to name just a few, spring readily to mind. Canada, too, still retains a friendship forged over many decades. Surprisingly, one of its most respected Premiers, William Lyon Mackenzie King, was a convinced Spiritualist who often sat with mediums. Indeed, they were even smuggled into his hotel suite when he visited London's bombed streets.

Moreover, King 'saw' visions in his shaving lather, as his personal diaries reveal. Some claim, and with justification, that he used a ouija board and a crystal ball for guidance in his personal life. The Prime Minister, who, it is said, did more to shape modern Canada than any other man, accepted spirit messages not only from his family, but another world leader, Franklin Roosevelt, the all-powerful President of the United States.

Despite the rigours of high office, King still found time to indulge his interest in psychic affairs. There is plenty of proof in his own words to support this belief. For example, he became friendly with Dr T. Glen Hamilton, probably Canada's most famous psychic researcher. He died some years ago.

Hamilton held over 1,000 test seances in fifteen years in his Winnipeg home. As a distinguished medical man, Hamilton practised for thirty years. For eleven of them he was a member of the Canadian Medical Association's national executive. An MP for five years, he also lectured at university level on clinical surgery.

The medic, a former sceptic, had a battery of fourteen cameras which simultaneously photographed various psychic phenomena. There were also three flashlights which were electrically fired. Hamilton's group included four medical men, two barristers, two engineers and a trained nurse. Three non-professional mediums were used. They were searched, like the sitters, before and after each seance. The researcher's unique collection of seance photos, records and documents is now housed at the University of Manitoba.

King's earlier diaries record the personal debt he felt to Dr Hamilton. On 27th August, 1933 King wrote: 'It is just a week ago that I was enjoying one of the most memorable experiences of my life as a guest of Mrs Hamilton and yourself. But what you are in yourselves, what you are achieving for science and religion and humanity, what you have received and recorded is what will afterwards be in my thoughts and remembrance.

'I had expected very much from what I heard of your researches from others, but the results surpassed all expectations. I cannot thank you and Mrs Hamilton enough for having taken me into your confidence and having permitted me to share in the very rich inheritance which is now yours. It does seem to me that you are all singularly blessed, and that through you a great blessing is about to be bestowed upon the world. Had I not seen the photographs you have, and heard from your lips what you read and told me, also had I not some previous experiences of my own and some knowledge of psychical science, I just could not have believed it was possible to proceed the lengths you have. I hope you will not fail to keep me in touch with your further discoveries. I shall always look back upon that day I spent with you as a place of new and higher beginning in my life and life's interest. I feel I have come to a new plane of existence myself. For such a gift, you will all realise adequate words of acknowledgement are not to be found.'

One of the communicators at the Hamilton seances was C. H. Spurgeon, the evangelist. Dr Hamilton sent King a booklet with quotations from Robert Louis Stevenson, a series of prayers written through an entranced medium.

On 29th September, 1933, King wrote praising spirit teachings he had heard through a medium at the Glen Hamilton home. He added: 'I am glad to have the photograph of the written script of Spurgeon's sermon. All this is amazing beyond words, but not in the least incredible once one sees it as the breaking forth of new light upon our realm of ignorance in regard to the spiritual forces at work about us.

'It is all so very simple and natural once one begins to admit its reality and genius. The world, however, has always rejected the simple things like Naaman of old, it does not want to be told to bathe in the

Water of Jordan, where they are close at hand; it wants pomp and miracles, the very things in which it professes not to believe.' Dr Hamilton died in 1935. When King heard of it, he sent the following letter on 26th November to Mrs Hamilton: 'You will not be surprised to know that I experience a very real sense of personal loss in the doctor's passing. Though we had met but once, and had shared little in the way of correspondence, I felt a very close attachment to him, and was as you know profoundly interested in his work in psychical research.

'I have looked upon him as one of the great pioneers in that field of thought and discovery. I now feel that not only our country but science, and even civilisation itself, has lost one of its great servants. Happily we have the faith which enables us to see the stars beyond the cypress trees . . . I can only hope that your sorrow may, ere this, have dissipated by the light of a wider knowledge and a profounder assurance of his continued presence at your side than could be possible to any save those who have shared the great experiences which you and he have shared . . .'

Mrs Hamilton later explained that for years the existence of the politician's letters was known among her own family and intimate friends, adding, 'We kept it quiet knowing that Mr King would have announced it had he wanted the information made public at the time.'

King first visited the Hamiltons as leader of the Liberal opposition. He arrived at 11 a.m., but his interest in what occurred was so engrossing he even risked missing his train that evening. 'Mr King,' said Mrs Hamilton, 'saw our photographs of the teleplasms which were photographed in our seance room. These included the face-likeness of C. H. Spurgeon and Raymond, son of Sir Oliver Lodge.'

Mrs Hamilton also recalled that King had a number of spirit writings read to him. These had been recorded by a secretary in the Hamilton seance room and came from the 'dead' Robert Louis Stevenson, author of *Treasure Island.*

Mrs Hamilton stated that King said during his Winnipeg visit he intended to write a book on his Spiritualist convictions and the foundations for them. In fact, he once approached a secretary with a view to engaging her to do the copy work.

'Mr King was not a Spiritualist in the popular sense,' Mrs Hamilton explained. 'He was a scientific investigator, and through his experience had come to believe in survival after death. His contact with his mother was not out of loneliness, but it was a great comfort to him.'

King's convictions are nowhere better expressed than in a letter he wrote to a little girl, Marilyn Kilbasco, who lived in his boyhood home, Woodside, in Kitchener, Ontario. Revisiting the home in the autumn of 1947 he met the child, then six, there. Shortly before Christmas in 1947, he learned that her father had died. His letter to Marilyn read in part: 'While we cannot see God, we have the story of the life of the little Christmas child to let us know what He is like. So I am perfectly sure that your dear father, while taken from you, has been taken to heaven where God Himself is, and that though you cannot see your dear father, he can see you and that his spirit will be watching over you and your mother and brothers and sisters at all times.

'When I was a little boy at Woodside, I found all this very difficult to comprehend, but as I have grown older, I have come to believe it more strongly every year, and I might say almost every day. So don't think of your father as gone. When you say your prayers, ask him, as well as God, to watch over you and to continue to care for you and your mother and all the family, and you will see by and by how, in some remarkable way, your prayers will be and have been answered . . .'

King was introduced to Spiritualism by the Marchioness of Aberdeen. She told him about American medium Etta Wreidt. The Premier met Mrs Wreidt through a mutual friend, the wife of a Liberal senator. Her father's will was missing. She consulted a medium, who told her it was in a chest of drawers in a house in France. And that is where she found it. So impressed was King with Mrs Wreidt that he invited her to his Kingsmere home for a summer visit.

He recorded these sittings in his diary. In one entry he wrote: 'I feel convinced of the survival beyond the grave of a spiritual body, of mind being the reality, but I am not convinced that all who are beyond are able yet to guide or dictate your conduct. They can do so only as they are entered into the highest while here below, or have progressed toward that highest in the beyond. Progression is not so rapid that much advance can be made in the period of a lifetime.'

Many of King's relatives and friends communicated from the Other Side. 'It would seem,' he stated, 'as if those we loved knew not only our behaviour but our spiritual needs, our thoughts, and were seeking mostly to administer to them.'

King, an austere Presbyterian, was convinced during his last year as Premier that he saw 'images' on his shaving lather. Again, these were described in his personal diary for 1948. It was opened by the

Government archives and released under the thirty-year ruling. King headed Canada's Liberal Party for twenty-nine years, being Premier for twenty-one. He retired in 1948, when seventy-four, and passed on in 1950. The first lather vision came on New Year's Eve. 'During shaving I looked at the lather and saw an extraordinary likeness to two dogs—quite perfect,' said the Premier.

King also thought there was another dog in the distance. The animals were Pat I and Pat II, former pet Scotch terriers, and a third dog he later received as a gift. On New Year's Day his lather contained a shape 'which was the most perfect head of my mother, again with two dogs. It was a particularly beautiful little image.' Later that January King saw an image of an eagle, a polar bear and a dog that 'might have been prophetic of what was happening in the struggle between Russia and the US.' This, of course, became known as the Cold War.

In the mid-1930s King sat with British medium Helen Hughes for the first time. She had no idea of the identity. One of the spirit voices Helen heard was a man's. He was the sitter's brother, a doctor, he insisted. Afterwards, the politician remarked, 'I know that was my brother. He spoke of things nobody else knew, nobody but the two of us.' He had passed in 1922.

Attending a social function at the former London Spiritualist Alliance, King told a distinguished group of Spiritualists he had received great help through mediumship. At another sitting with Helen Hughes, he praised her gift warmly, saying he knew no one who had given greater comfort 'or has done more valuable war work.' He told her he regularly received communications from his mother and brother through other psychic sources.

A bachelor, King had a deep love for his mother, who passed in 1917. He kept her portrait in his study. Night and day a light burned before the painting, and fresh flowers and a cross were placed there.

Helen Hughes was his medium for fourteen years. At one of his last meetings with her, he said: 'Well, Helen Hughes, of all the people I have met, I do not think I can pay a better tribute to any of them than I can to you for the work you have done in proving Survival in these war days. You will never know what it meant to many people. The people who knew nothing of this thing have not yet begun to live!' Later in 1947 the Premier told a graduating class of lawyers: 'I believe deeply in personal survival. I believe the spirits of those we love are around us at this time.'

Of King's visits to Mrs Hughes, she commented: 'It was as if he had his mother living over here in Britain. What would any son do if he came here on business? He'd look her up. He'd want to see her and talk to her. He didn't want her advice about public affairs, for he knew more about them than she did. He wanted to know how she was, whom she had with her. He wanted to talk about family matters.'

The medium could not recall one instance when there was any mention of public affairs. But he was warned about his retirement from public life. Said Helen: 'At least three years before he died his mother told him he was doing too much, his heart wouldn't stand it. He took her advice in the end, but not soon enough.'

Helen Hughes recollected King's first visit to her, in the early 1930s. 'I had no idea who he was,' she stated. 'They don't tell us, you know. All I knew was that a man would be coming for a sitting at 10.30 in the morning. He just came in and sat down without saying anything.

'One of the voices I heard was from a man who said he was his brother. Mr King wanted to be told something about him. It came through that he was a doctor. After a while I got the name, Mac. He said a lot about the family—he'd say, "Do you remember, Willie, when we were children, do you remember so-and-so?" After it was over Mr King said: "I know that was my brother. He spoke of things nobody else knew, nobody but the two of us."'

Through Helen Hughes and Hester Dowden, an automatic writing medium, King got in touch not only with his family but also with his beloved Irish terrier, Pat. Mrs Hughes once reported to him: 'Your sister is here, and she has a beautiful dog with her. The dog doesn't seem to have been very long over there.' King was greatly impressed and told her a story he had related to many friends in Ottawa. The night before Pat died, his watch fell off his bedside table 'for no apparent reason.' He found it in the morning face down on the floor, with the hands stopped at 4.20. 'I am not psychic,' King said, 'but I knew then, as if a voice were speaking to me, that Pat would die before another twenty-four hours went by.' That night the faithful Pat got out of his basket with a last effort, climbed up on his master's bed, and died there. King looked at his watch. It was 4.20.

King's diaries also reveal that he not only experienced prophetic dreams but visions, which he regarded as of a higher order. In these his dead mother or some other guardian spirit appeared to give guidance, but never to attempt to influence his political decisions.

When the Premier was lying seriously ill in 1948 at the Dorchester Hotel, London, he received few visitors. News reporters waiting in the hotel lobby saw King George VI, Winston Churchill and Pandit Nehru. Then, to their surprise, two unknown women were shown to the Prime Minister's suite. Their visit lasted fifty minutes. The women were medium Geraldine Cummins and her colleague, Miss Gibbes.

Through her superb automatic writing, Geraldine wrote pages of messages purporting to come from the Premier's mother and brother and Franklin Roosevelt. One message described how the 'dead' President of the United States had met Mr King's mother in the spirit world. The Canadian Premier commented, 'The phrases he used, the characterisation, were exactly what I'd have expected from Franklin Roosevelt if he'd met my mother in life.'

Though the Premier received, via Helen Hughes, a warning from his mother at least three years before he passed that he was doing too much work, other advice was given by Mr Roosevelt through Geraldine Cummins.

'Don't retire,' beseeched the ex-President, 'stay on the job. Your country needs you there. I am most uneasy. You can put my mind at rest. I learned that you might consider retiring. I beg of you at whatever cost to continue in public life. It is wiser from the point of view of your health to retire, but I feel it is your duty not merely to your country, but to the world to stay on.

'I want you to retain Canada's independence. There is a bunch of roughnecks in finance in the USA. They would like to get hold of Canada through economic penetration . . . I don't want big business later on to get undue control of Canada.'

The American spirit communicator went on: 'Mac, you know the old saying. The nineteenth century was the century of USA. The twentieth century will be Canada's century. That is, in my opinion, far more likely to come true if you remain in public life some years longer.

'Don't let those doctrinaire theorists in the English Government get hold of you either and pass their theories on to you. Keep your independence of thought, but get all the men you can from the mother or grandmother country to settle in Canada.

'It will be in the interests of both countries, for, later on, I see a population difficulty in England and a lot of discontent. In fact England's future gives me more of a headache than that of France. France will eventually get through by means of strong leadership. Their leader won't be a pleasant fellow, but he will get them on their feet. England will be more difficult. Her nervous system—I mean of her people—is out of gear. There will be trouble later for the English cabinet.'

At another sitting in October 1948, the communicator said to be Roosevelt warned that the danger of war lay in Asia. The Berlin airlift, which then seemed important, was merely a side issue, but there would be war in the Far East within two years, he asserted.

The communicator was apparently right. In 1961, Miss Cummins revealed that a Canadian, Mr Patrick, called on her to examine the original automatic script she had written for Mackenzie King. The visitor told her, with great emotion, that because Mr King ignored the message, American big business was 'well on its way to control of Canada.' He exclaimed to the medium, 'My God, the foresight of FDR seeing this situation eleven years before it happened!'

Miss Cummins considered this as one of three 'nobody knows facts' in the script. The second was the coming of de Gaulle as ruler of France. The third, 'war in the Far East,' mentioned by the communicator two years before it happened, apparently referred to the Korean conflict, following the success of the Communists in China.

Miss Cummins and her friend were smuggled into the Premier's presence more than once. On one occasion they called on him at his hotel during one of his many wartime visits to London. Eager journalists, hearing about his interest in psychics, gathered to intercept and interview the mediums with whom he sat. To avoid them, King, recovering from a temporary ailment, sat up in bed while Geraldine Cummins used an invalid table to receive her automatic writing. When they had finished, the table was restored to its former position, complete with its vase of flowers, so that the curious nurse in attendance would not learn about the secret sitting.

Other messages through the medium's hand were said to come from Canadian leaders. Mr King's mentor and friend Sir Wilfrid Laurier, W. S. Fielding and Sir Oliver Mowat were among them. Miss Cummins said she had heard of none of these men.

King once wrote to Geraldine: 'There can be no truer explanation of the terrible conditions through which the world has recently been passing, and is still suffering from, than the conflict of materialism and spiritual interpretation of life. Like you, but in a different way, I have sought to wage war on the former, and shall continue to do so to the end.'

Others, too, have claimed psychic links with King. A Montreal medium, Mrs Wilder, told a fellow Canadian that she was booked once a week all during the war for a seance with the politician, who went to Ottawa for that purpose alone. She was also consulted by President Roosevelt, and flew to Washington weekly, she said.

Shortly before his death, King mentioned to an acquaintance something he said President Roosevelt had told him only a day or so before. Thinking this was a slip, the friend tactfully, and not surprisingly, suggested Mr King meant President Truman. No said the ex-Premier. He had been conversing with the 'dead' President Roosevelt. They frequently chatted in that way, he added.

Some of the striking results of Miss Cummins's seances, King agreed, should be published in one of Geraldine's books. He promised to contribute. Sadly, before her book, *Unseen Adventures,* was ready the Premier passed.

Geraldine arranged for the galley proofs concerning this material to be sent to his executors. She received a frantic cable that they were coming to see her. With threats and persuasion, one of them tried to force her to omit the account. He was afraid publication might influence Canadian Roman Catholics to vote against his Party. Geraldine Cummins refused point blank. However, when news of King's Spiritualist interests leaked out, it caused a sensation. If it had been known in his lifetime, it is thought he would probably never have won the votes of the French-Canadian Catholics, which tipped the electoral scales to make him Prime Minister for over two decades.

Subsequently, when a Canadian magazine refuted stories in *Psychic News* that King had sought guidance in state affairs, corroboration was at hand.

Miss Lind-af-Hageby, a crusader for animal rights, was an inseparable friend of the Duchess of Hamilton.

Miss Lind categorically stated: 'The "inner man" of Mr Mackenzie King was animated by Spiritualism, by the knowledge of survival and communication, by knowledge of the powers of prophecy and—in the innermost part of his inner man—by his profound and enduring love of his mother. It is not possible that a man can go so deeply into Spiritualism as Mackenzie King did, apart from sittings with mediums and receiving personal messages, without this colouring his actions as a statesman and his judgement of world events.'

Miss Lind first met the Premier in Geneva in 1936, where she and the Duchess of Hamilton founded the International Humanitarian Bureau in an effort to stimulate the League of Nations to accept the extension of justice to animals as part of the movement for world peace. The women saw King frequently, and had many talks on Spiritualism.

When he expressed a wish to meet London Spiritualists, Miss Lind, then president of the London Spiritualist Alliance, arranged a party for him to meet mediums. He even visited their homes.

Said Miss Lind, 'To us who attended practically every general assembly of the League of Nations in Geneva, who met many statesmen who had come as delegates, the fact that Mr Mackenzie King sought guidance in statecraft—which really amounts to lifecraft—and acted upon it was perfectly plain.'

Travelling in Time

PROBABLY THE MAJORITY of individuals regard clairvoyants as fat, fey women, dispensing homely Other World advice and communications to gullible females, in 'short offering to the public a sort of psychic tea and sympathy service. Nothing could be further from the truth. In a sense mediums live in two worlds simultaneously. It is not an easy life by any means.

Even today mediums are still regarded with a certain frivolity, the butt of many an old, tired music hall joke. Yet clairvoyants and the like can somehow escape the world of five senses and time travel. Such a case revolves around a seer who not only foresaw who would be the country's Premier, but correctly predicted the outcome of various battles.

During the Russian-Polish conflict after the First World War, Polish medium Madame Przybylska 'heard' messages. Recorded at seances—these were attended·by friends—in June and July 1920, the communications referred to forthcoming events in July and August of the same year. At that time the Polish forces were holding every front whilst the Bolsheviks were retreating. But on 10th June, 1920, the medium received the following communication:

'The Council of Ministers is not yet constituted, but sooner or later you will hear of Witos. What misfortunes! What disasters! How many dead on your battlefields! A disaster to your troops. During this month there will be a great change in the Council. Witos will be Prime Minister. A greater man than your ministers will give you help. In August everything will change. A stranger arrives, with whom Pildsudki will take counsel; he will have much influence. The systematic strikes will come to an end. Towards the middle of August you will see that your misfortunes change.'

The medium was soon to be proved dramatically correct. On 28th

June, the Bolsheviks began a totally unexpected offensive on the northern front. The Polish army lost its ground in Munich, Vilna and Lida. Though Warsaw came under threat, as the medium foretold, it was never invaded.

On 12th July the medium sat for a group of the capital's society figures. Part of the message received stated: 'Lenin's power grows. A flood of men invades your country. You abandon your fields. But be fearless. I bless your town. The disaster is only on the right bank of the Vistula. All will change for the better.'

In August, as the medium stated, the Poles claimed victory. Furthermore, the 'stranger' referred to did manifest in the flesh. This was General Weygand, who did counsel Pildsudki. Witos, mentioned in the 10th June communication, did become Poland's premier, though he was, until then, a political non-entity. Had she lived longer it is interesting to muse whether Madame Przybylska would have foretold Poland's fierce Second World War battles, the end of its democracy and the start of Communist rule. That was to spell the death knell to Poland's psychic life, once so rich, now so poor.

Turning the clock back further proof definitely exists that Napoleon III and his wife received dramatic—indeed astonishingly evidential—seance-room proofs from celebrated Victorian medium D. D. Home.

Picture the scene. The year is 1857. The month is February. On the 13th of that month Home was presented to the couple at the Tuileries. Besides several in attendance on the Emperor, the Empress was present with her entourage. At the medium's request a number were asked to leave. Offended, and upstaged, the Empress flounced from the room. One who remained behind was Prince Murat, the King of Naples' son. Supernormal phenomena occurred almost immediately, even though the Emperor was sceptical. As the table levitated into the air, Prince Murat took to his knees and grasped Home's feet. By this time impressed, the Emperor said he would like his wife to see the supernormal proceedings. Indeed, he personally went to fetch her. Still put out that her entourage had been banished, the Empress nonetheless complied with her husband's request. The table, she told her sister, moved and shivered. Home, she explained, 'sits with his hand on the table top. He sits alongside the table. As you can well imagine we had first assured ourselves that he had nothing to do with what was happening.'

What also impressed the Empress was that when she asked

questions mentally they were correctly replied by spirit raps. At one point during the seance, the medium requested her to feel under the table. Obviously, he had psychic pre-knowledge of what was about to occur. It shattered the Empress. Doing as requested, tears filled her eyes. For underneath the table she felt her dead father's temporarily materialised hand. But how did the Empress know with utter certainty it was not some cruel, contrived seance-room trick? In answer to her husband's question how could she be sure, the Empress replied: 'There was a defect in one of the fingers . . . just as there was in life.' To satisfy himself the Emperor too felt the hand, along with its evidential defect.

More was to come. At a third seance held in the Salon Louis Quinze paper and pencil were laid on the table in advance in case any spirit messages came. They did. All the sitters witnessed the appearance of a small materialised hand. It took the pencil and wrote a single word, 'Napoleon.' The signature was without doubt that of the great Napoleon himself. The Empress asked to kiss the hand. It moved first to her lips and then to her husband's. Not surprisingly soon all Paris was agog with accounts of the Emperor's seances.

So impressed was the Empress with Home that she offered to take the education of the medium's young sister, Christine, into her own hands. The offer was accepted. Christine was educated at the noted Convent of the Sacred Heart where the Empress was a pupil. For while she wished the medium's sister to be educated in matters of life, Home had well and truly educated her in matters of death . . . and the Beyond.

As with John Brown and Queen Victoria, Court circles were increasingly outraged at the Emperor's psychic connections. Indeed, the Minister of Foreign Affairs made his views perfectly clear. He threatened to quit his post unless Home was banished from the Court. The Emperor stood firm. However, never again did the medium hold seances at the Tuileries, the French court's official seat. Nonetheless, still he was to enjoy Royal patronage and friendship on both sides of the grave.

Here it is apposite to include one of the most amazing seance-room claims ever: that Queen Astrid of Belgium materialised and was even photographed after she died. Astrid, who bore her husband three children, Baudouin, Albert and Josephine-Charlotte, was not only strikingly beautiful but much-loved by the people. None is immune from tragedy, not even royalty. In the first year of the new King's reign, the Queen was killed in a road crash. To add to his pain, her husband, King Leopold, was driving the car.

Before her marriage Astrid was Crown Princess of Sweden being, as she was, a niece of the King of Sweden. It was in Copenhagen in 1939 that she was to make her alleged spirit return. When the Queen was killed at Lucerne, Switzerland, her husband was grief-stricken. The world mourned the passing of a gracious, charming woman. The medium through whom Astrid supposedly showed herself was Einar Nielsen. His psychic gifts attracted the attention of a leading German psychic researcher with the unlikely name of Baron Schrenck Notzing.

Queen Astrid's apperances at seances was witnessed by many Spiritualists. A photograph of the materialised monarch was taken by Martin Liljeblad, a Swedish clergyman. He testified in a book to the remarkable phenomena he witnessed.

Liljeblad, a member of the State Church in Helsingborg, wrote his book in direct defiance of the Church authorities. He first became interested in psychic matters in the late 1930s after sitting with a medium in Copenhagen. The cleric was so impressed that he engaged a Danish medium and hired halls in different cities in Sweden for Spiritualist meetings. This psychic spoke in trance, giving, it is said, messages from Astrid.

Because of his book and the meetings, Liljeblad was sentenced to two months' suspension from the Church without pay. There were even attempts to get him certified as insane, but these failed. The ecclesiastical court which imposed the suspension had no power to curb his Spiritualist activities. Liljeblad continued his meetings without mediums. It was in his second book, *My Meetings with Friends of the Light,* that the minister told of his seances with Einar Nielsen at which Queen Astrid materialised.

Two Swedish Spiritualists who had frequent sittings with Nielsen and saw the Queen appear were interviewed by *Psychic News.* About twenty sitters, they said, were present. Liljeblad used three cameras and took his pictures simultaneously with a white flash after obtaining permission from the medium's guide. Queen Astrid spoke in Swedish. One of the visitors told *Psychic News* she had sometimes sat with the medium in a corner of the room which was curtained off to form a cabinet; she had seen spirit beings build up while she held the medium's hands and walked out of the cabinet with a materialised spirit being, leaving the medium inside. Once, she claimed, a materialisation helped her carry a chair from the cabinet while the entranced medium was still inside.

At that time it was freely rumoured among London Spiritualists that King Leopold was a Spiritualist at heart and frequently visited Britain to sit with a medium and talk to his dead wife. At any event, when Astrid died, a Mrs A. Stuart of Bristol sent him a copy of her book, *No More Tears*, in which she described how Spiritualism comforted her after her son died. She thought the King would derive some help from it in the sorrow of his bereavement. Mrs Stuart, it is said, received a letter from Leopold saying he was deeply affected by reading the book.

Did Leopold know of his wife's spirit appearances? That we shall never know. For it seems that when dead Kings—and Queens—speak, an element of mystery nearly always remains.

Index